I Con

TIM THORNE has written twelve collections of poetry, has edited four anthologies and his poems have appeared in most major Australian literary journals. He established the Tasmanian Poetry Festival and was its Director for 17 years. He has performed his work throughout Australia and overseas, and has worked as a poet in a variety of community contexts. He lives in Launceston, Tasmania, with his wife Stephanie and a large garden.

I Con

New and Selected Poems

Tim Thorne

Cambridge

PUBLISHED BY SALT PUBLISHING
PO Box 937, Great Wilbraham, Cambridge CB21 5JX United Kingdom

All rights reserved

© Tim Thorne, 2008

The right of Tim Thorne to be identified as the
author of this work has been asserted by him in accordance
with Section 77 of the Copyright, Designs and Patents Act 1988.

This book is in copyright. Subject to statutory exception
and to provisions of relevant collective licensing agreements,
no reproduction of any part may take place without the written
permission of Salt Publishing.

Salt Publishing 2008

Printed and bound in the United Kingdom by Biddles Ltd, King's Lynn, Norfolk

Typeset in Swift 9.5 / 13

*This book is sold subject to the conditions that it shall not,
by way of trade or otherwise, be lent, re-sold, hired out,
or otherwise circulated without the publisher's prior consent
in any form of binding or cover other than that in which
it is published and without a similar condition including this
condition being imposed on the subsequent purchaser.*

ISBN 978 1 84471 337 0 hardback

Salt Publishing Ltd gratefully acknowledges
the financial assistance of Arts Council England

1 3 5 7 9 8 6 4 2

Contents

Emoh Ruo	1
POEMS 1968–1973	3
Star	5
Hustler	11
High Country	12
Sideflower	14
Voyage of the Eye	15
Whatever Happened to Conway Twitty?	17
Launceston	18
Highway	20
Somewhere Between Waxahachie and Woonsocket	21
Advice to a Popular Hero	25
Man and Law	26
Sydney's Drowning	28
Western Addition	29
California	32
Elegy for Jenny	33
Aubade	34
Autumn	35
POEMS 1974–1979	39
Grammar	41
Jet Lag	42
Squad	43
Roulette	44
Five Trees	45
Clare	48
Bag of Shit	49
80° 08' 1934	50

Polheim	51
The Worst Journey in the World	52
Onyx River	53
Mawson Alone	54
Growth	55
Melody for a Hard Summer	56
Underground	58
Vanzetti	59
Blade	60
Bolt	61
Song for Seychelles	62

from THE ATLAS (1982) — 65

I	67
II	68
III	71
V	72
Interlude (The boy running . . .)	75
VII	76
XIII	78
XIV	80
Interlude (By the Greystone bed . . .)	83
XVI	84
XIX	85

POEMS 1980–1989 — 87

Left	89
Fluid	90
Low Tide, North Esk	91
Brady's Lookout	92
Macquarie House	94
Reds	95

Bane	97
Tight	98
To Ashes	99
On/Against the Wall	100
Launching, By George	101
Petty Sessions	102
Songs of the Protest Era	104
from THE STREETS AREN'T FOR DREAMERS (1995)	105
The Cull	107
Rat's Song	108
Stage Dive	109
Roadkill	110
Advice	111
Words for K	112
Bouncer	113
Escort	114
Busking	115
Arriving in Devonport	117
Bear	118
from TAKING QUEEN VICTORIA TO INVERESK (1997)	119
Comrade Revenant	121
The Last Muster of the Aborigines at Risdon	122
Low Tide	123
Fruit and Flowers	124
Sunday in the Gardens	126
Naming the Sensation No 2	127
Humpty Dumpty and Taxidermy	129
Sydney Cove	130
Bound to Please	131
Led	132

Poems 1990–1999   133
   Leipzig   135
   To Adrian Paunescu   136
   Crash   139
   The Living are Left with Imagined Lives   140
   Cold War   141
   When the Saints Go Marching Out   142
   Love Poem for Stephanie   143
   Don Gibson and Etymology   144
   Erechtheus 33's Apologia   145
   Poem for Port Arthur   146
   Aerodynamics   147
   Speaking for Myself   148
   The Aisles   149
   Brontë Country   151
   Mother and Son   152
   For My Father   153
   Keeping the Dream Alive   155

from aUStralia (2004)   157
   Oosutoraria   159
   Vinegar Hill   161
   Pinchgut   162
   Spider Dance and Horse Whip   163
   Mandarin of the Crystal Button   164
   Coningham v Coningham   165
   Black Cat and Wooden Shoe   166
   Lockout   167
   The Mayor   168
   Tanah Merah   169
   Advent: 21 Dec. 1967   170
   Sight Screen   171

POEMS 2000–2006 173
   Et in Acadia Ego? 175
   Dry 177
   Zig-Zag Track 178
   Scapeland 179
   Writing the World 180
   Meditation on Parliament House, Canberra, 2002 . 181
   Elegance 182
   Chemically Sharpened 183
   Mesopotamian Suite 184
   South-Western Baptist 191
   Meditations on Ms Westbury's Precepts 192
   Celebritocracy 193
   Dentist's Waiting Room 195
   Red Label 196
   There are No Kangaroos in Austria 198
   Elegy for Sandra Dee (1942–2005) 199
   Dolphins Off Sikinos 200
   The Death of Reason 201
   Roncesvalles: Men at Work 202

from TRAINSTATIONS FROM EUROPEAN POETS . . 203
   The Bawd, the Lair and Albert Ross 205
   Do We Know Elly Gee? 206
   An Evening in the Trakl Night Club 207
   Stone No 5: Osip and the Minor Celebrity 208

from A LETTER TO EGON KISCH (2007) 209
   from section II 211
   from section VIII 214

   Notes 219

Acknowledgements

Poems in this selection have appeared in the following books:

Tense Mood and Voice (Lyre-Bird Writers, Sydney, 1969)
The What of Sane (Prism Books, Sydney, 1971)
New Foundations (Prism Books, Sydney, 1976)
A Nickel In My Mouth (Robin Hill Books, Flowerdale, 1979)
The Atlas (Black Lightning Press, Wentworth Falls, 1982)
Red Dirt (Paper Bark Press, Sydney, 1990)
The Sreets Aren't for Dreamers (Shoestring Press, Nottingham, 1995)
Taking Queen Victoria to Inveresk (QVM&AG, Launceston, 1997)
Head and Shin (Walleah Press, Hobart, 2004)
Best Bitter (PressPress, Berry, 2006)
A Letter to Egon Kisch (Cornford Press, Launceston, 2007)

as well as a number of journals both hard copy and online.

Emoh Ruo

My poems are cladding,
washable, weatherproof.
What is inside is not
just a home; it's a house.

A white tyre is a swan
is a metaphor. En-
jambements roll, wagon wheels.
Stanzas are garden beds.

Structure and patterning
need tough material:
vinyl and pebble-dash,
birdseye maple veneer.

Reader, wipe your feet on
my jokey welcome mat.
Come in. Get comfortable.
Mi casa su casa.

It's more than a building,
more than a collection;
it's an investment in
iconic literature.

Poems 1968–1973

Star

for Stephanie

Proem

1.

You laugh at me behind your face
and twist the last ace out of your frilly sleeve.
I lose. I leave.

2.

The prisoners exercise in cages,
insane, concentric cricket nets.
No-one rages. Everyone plots.

3.

There are many things I lack,
but I'll get my own back later on.
Just wait, baby, I'll learn
every trick in the book, fly-leaf to colophon.

Amphetamine hands will cover your eyes.
Scintillating fingernails will rip your lace,
but that will be only in your brain.
I'll come up from behind.
My mind will blow your mind,
baby.
And it won't be me but my poetry
that blows in your belly.

I shall walk for you,
walk through a continent of streets
yard by dry yard
and wet,
through a string of cities

avoiding the cracks
for your sake.
I shall make
each step in praise of you:
the slow blow,
the controlled explosion of your complexion
and your composure, the skilled destruction
of every plane and crease
in your photogenic face,
baby.

Sequence

Each separate town is slapped on the highway like
a hoarding, vulgar as a teenage laugh.
Milkbars, town hall, rec. and cenotaph,
two pubs with snooker tables, public dyke
—interior: pale green semigloss (by the shire)
and thick, white coin-scratch (by the Baptist choir).

Slogans and flags wave from each service station
like some third world republic crude with pride.
Deep in those shabby, chrome milkbars I've plied
the jukeboxes with dud coins to saturation
or in the soft air of the saloon bars
sent the reds spinning like unruly stars.

Bold in studded leather I've played it cool;
aphrodisiac hamburgers and cokes
have led to furtive, half-successful pokes
under the pine trees down behind the school.
Then always the big wheelspin, the muffler gone,
the next raw town to burn. Clear out. Move on.

CRYSTAL PALACE

Cock of so many country towns, so sure,
I, who have sent so many spherical phrases
rolling for fluke breaks over the green cloth,
rhymes dropping into sweet, symmetrical pockets,
I have felt the poem grabbing at my guts,
the pen in my hand like a cue nestling into chalk
smoothly, despite the heavy breathing. Calm,
I have planned to avoid the easy eight-ball image
and have had in my head all the relevant intricate angles.

But my bitch of a muse is in league with a hustler:
prick-teasing stocking-tops at the saloon door,
every trick of the slicker with brylcreem hair
taking the simple lair for a ride
inside the bars of the city I want to love.
(The cage is merely a pun, therefore a cage,
a trap for the simple lair on every page.)
I want to love the city. I want to screw
her rolling grey in the sun. I want to screw
her cheap in the night with her neon hair. I want
that girl on the bus, busting out of her skirt for it,
the break that never ends, the one two-bob
that keeps the jukebox going till it melts.

Why should I always be the simple lair?
Why should I always wear
my poems like a shoestring tie?
My hair
too long, my pimples pointing to the sky?
The sky, it is true,
is always Mitchell blue.
I don't know why.

(Beware
of anything they offer you.
Beware of the con-man's swy.
Take care in Sydney, yeah.
Ooh,
they're
sly.)

After the killing you can only grin,
walk out, walk home. Desire has been taken away
along with your roll. Hundreds of empty cars
move down the empty streets. You cannot fill
the city with your braggadocio.
The simple grin has its own cunning, slides
values around like sheets of paper, so:
"Put it all down to experience."
"Your father could have told you so."
A fool and his cliches soon are parted from
the truth. The truth is you are beaten, broke.
She's kicked you out with your balls in a fiery knot.
The ram slips sheepishly, lopsided, off.

(Avoid the grin
inevitably inane.
If you can't win,
then don't stick out your chin;
some bastard'll hit it again.
Pack in
the down-but-not-out, thin,
brave, callow grin.
Grab pain.)

PAIN.

1.

The street lies out, inviting,
the flat of a large-bladed knife.
Slap your soles on it, test its temper.
think of the edge, dwell on it, dwell on it.

There at the tip a street-light drips.
I think of all the vulnerable parts
of the human body, throat and wrists,
baby-soft hollows between ribs and hips.

2.

In my room I find twenty-one cents in change
scattered among the cheap, essential furniture.
It's nearly ten. It's worth the risk.
The pub is just two blocks away.

Calm down. Breathe slow and flex your fist.
Before I've finished my beer a drunk's thrown out
protesting. "But it's payday. I can pay!
Look!" I don't need to look. I follow him,

sure and dark, into a lane. "Got a light?"
One punch . . . a plastic wallet—twenty quid
and a crumpled photo of him with five kids.
Calm down. I suppose his wife works, anyway.

Envoi

Baby, I've shown you what I mean by art.
I've made it at last here on the big-town scene.
Sure, I've been conned and hustled but I'd been
too big too long back home. Look, kid, I'm smart.
I've got a ring with a real garnet and I wear
real sharp suits, dark socks. I know the score.
You won't be laughing at me any more.
You wouldn't recognise the country lair.
I realise now it wasn't only you
I had to get even with. I had to strike
back hard at all of them till I came through
with words that screamed louder than any bike,
louder than anything on the hit parade,
but true, but true. Baby, I've got it made.

Hustler

If you must trick my spinning, trick it out
with the trappings of death, gaily: silver chains—
each link a bell, light in any wind
against a black caparison.

                      You know
there's a man in Callan Park with insane hair,
locked up because he tried to write one line
of poetry.

                Shoot pool: you're halfway there.
But the face of your ex-girlfriend's lover says,
"Don't try to hustle. Look across the bay.
See the *Empress* lit up like a mine."
Everyone's a guard. They'll never let
you even toss for break.

                          If you must trick
me when I'm skilful, do it with a flair,
otherwise the doctors and the screws
won't even understand why I am there.

High Country

1. Homecoming

Button-grass flats, pale through the drizzle: my eyes
unhinged, unhingeing; patch-brown pools:
my body's own still liquids.

After the climb, hard through the spine's country,
where the leatherwood and myrtle drip
holes into the bent flesh,

after the droplets running off the tight skin
around the vein-riddled gullies
stretched on a hairpin bend,

this is the homecoming, arriving at this level—
the brain laid open in the wet,
nerve ends like sags, open.

2. The Hut

The plastic strips flap in the doorway still,
sad alchemical colours to ward off evil.
The poet comes home like a blue-arsed fly
too late for the real summer, too soon
for the winds that take the corner of the year
on two loud tyres—the screech of March.

I light the fire and wait for my life's details
to dry out—buckled paperbacks,
the sleeve of an early Dylan record
(young jew-angel's face, cowboy mystery,
holding his guitar's neck like a flowering tree).
A man could die waiting between these hills.

Outside in gumboots, moving rocks around,
channelling off the water, watching it take
used-up petals like brain cells with it, down
to the flats where my brackish eyes are set like traps,
I am immune here, acting without itch,
connections all leached, open, waiting.
One day, too late for insects, bleak with peace,
after a month of my turning stones by the moon,
the hills will hear the brash harmonica
and send a patly scored reply in gusts.
And in that instant as the axis tilts
someone will cross the sags, his clothes blown dry.

Sideflower

Your highway body,
my love a sideflower
indigo-petalled like a
jealous kiss.

That married bastard mauled your
ringfinger.

I wore my red scarf over the Shoalhaven
and saw how sadly straight the
road was.

Voyage of the Eye

I

A short, uneven fingernail
scratches the surface of the eye.
The motors start. The big screw
turns to flood the ignorant air.
We have known many voyages;
some well. Some we've only read of
on the wall-posters/covering roughnesses,
balancing on the breath of the people/
seemed the most real. But this one,
planned in the holy, forgotten centre
of the maze,/but this one, comrades/
prepared where the dusty red trucks pull up
for fish on the broken wharf, this one
(as you will see) is unique in its
reality. Eyelashes intermesh.
The hull's long shudder slides into
the incipient vision of velocity.

II

Where are your children, senator?
The municipal playing gronds are curved
like the planet Earth. The lava underneath
pushes two pubescent silhouettes
against the hollow silver of the sky:
your children./Death comes confidently soft
in the eggshell of evening./Where are the people?
And you had left the comfort of your maze
long before the thin chemical line
traced through the pot-bellies, leaving
artificial pus. Was it only
to arrange this trip? Or did you know

your children, knowing that the heavy shadow
of the flowering gum would provide, would provide?
And children are of the people./Read the sign,
the promulgation/We dare not disembark.

III

Another blink of the automatic eye:
the gases from the legitimate lab slide out,
greet roses in the dying afternoon.
The patients are walked, slowly, past the signs
that stake the candidates' hearts into the soil.
The Central Committee/That's enough now, nurse;
my cardigan/met this morning/Turn
that damn thing off/through the streets, they said,
the streets/That rose: no wonder they call it
Peace/the Secretary/my cardigan/
the last poster/The damn machines
have taken over. See that tube;
it's growing. Peace. Good afternoon.

IV

That was a memorable voyage, child.
The pages of the diary are turned.
The senator welcomed us where old men
still spit their dreams over the rail.
We're safe. The bloodshot television
can't be turned off, but all hale breath
belongs to the people. The people are tired.
They slowly kill the image on the screen.

Whatever Happened to Conway Twitty?

My bakelite mantle set pulled him in
through the whine and crackle of KZ and I
drummed on a dented pencil tin
to *Danny Boy* or *Mona Lisa,*
tensing my hands and jaw as his art
made seven syllables of "heart".

Five p.m. was too early to get
anything like a good reception
and I broke the volume knob off that set
trying to bring America closer,
or if not America, then at least
Stan the Man, oracle and priest.

Masturbation and vandalism
came with darkness, but first the radio
would spurt its sweet, commercial chrism,
the god would descend through static, lift up, up,
up to the top of the *Cashbox* chart
all seven syllables of my heart.

Launceston

Planted in patches, missing the steeper slopes
and the flood-plains and occasionally
leaving a col surprisingly bare
to the cold sky, rolled around your three
rivers like a fog, you have grown
out of a photo in *National Geographic*
of a town (Pop. 683) on Kamchatka.
A hundred times bigger than Kikhchik,
you have its air of utter subservience
to the lonelier of the winds, the desolate aeroplanes.

Only, on Sunday nights, in a tight rotation
of attics, some three dozen brains
are picked by a culture's plectrums till
a sour rhythm is forced through the sweet
smoke of pot and incense. Dylan lives!
Outside, FJs are dragging up the street.

At lunchtimes you can read all the signs
more clearly. Jesus saves! Bank on the Wales!
Drive-in! Give way! You know they weren't decreed
by the men who painted them or drove the nails.
Below them sit two rows of foundry workers.
The evangelist, the manager, the cop
panic where the footpath has become
a slippery gauntlet. You could hear a sandwich drop.
But someone speeds past in a white Mercedes.
There are some gods that nobody can reach.

Don't complain because the town is always waiting,
because a twelve-string on its own can't teach.
Don't yearn so vaguely for a revolution.

Walk up the hills, running your finger along
the fences. Get to know the quainter gables.
See how sandstone and fibro both belong.
Roam suburbs like divisions of your mind.
Especially, react with quiet candour;
a town can neither rant nor lie. A guitar
changes nothing, whatever colour,
whatever blues you play, unless you play it.
And candlesmoke has filled the windows in,
so no-one outside is allowed to care.

And as for the other, follow all the in-
structions patiently, paying close attention
to the width of the bottle's neck, the type of wick,
the distance of the throw required. Choose
the time carefully. Split his blond-brick
house and brick-blonde wife without emotion.
Freedom's not a very abstract notion.

Highway

The sun aches.
My diesel head has
the knowledge of smiles
that knock. Fuel/need is somewhere
like a flake/is a shining giveaway.

Methedrine and bitumen
pave the way/torn cans
flash/and all the backs that built it:
Balmain guernseys bent in the rain/I am
bruised between midday and gravel edges.

High in the cab/Christ,
the sky's so loud/what are
the DMR doing in my spine?
Exhaust/various metallic colours: my vertebrae are the broken
white line.

Somewhere Between Waxahachie and Woonsocket

1

Somewhere between Waxahachie and Woonsocket
somebody dies. Cleanly,
something slides into a
life like a liquid into the
fuel tank of a Saturn.

Of course, it's never that simple
but the actions of twenty thousand everydays
are all timed keenly
by the blade in the brain
and are calculated for the big moon-shot.

Buried under the black wax soil
of the south-eastern quarter of the USA
there is a large computerised plant
where it all works.
Think of the potential there

for imagery—pocket watch
which is really a heart; the gold
of Fort Knox; the fallout shelter
beneath the White House; steam
issuing under the Oracle's tripod;

stainless steel hell; wonders of surgery.
But think, mostly, of what above all
this wired womb goes on
and what, at times on the conscious earth,
stops going on.

2

When my uncle died I was kind of
awkward; at twelve I was awkward anyway.
But after the first dislocation,
after the mystery of seeing
a grown man lie down and grunt
and piss himself in the middle of a ball game,
after Dad and Uncle Pat had come
to attend to whatever it is
that men attend to at such times,
I took my young cousins round to the back yard
and furiously played kick-for-kick with them
against the cement wall. I joked loudly.
They laughed. Then I caught cousin Libby's eye
through the dining-room window. I tried
to show her in one look
that I knew why she was crying
but that I had a job to do.

3

Watch out for the bare wire,
for the spark in the cracked socket.
Kneeling, you are vulnerable; down
by the skirting-board, aware
of the volume of the room behind you,
of the space you occupied standing.

A second ago you knew all
the secrets of power. The future
was clean as the moon.

The present moment is liftoff.

4

Memento mori. Don't forget
to keep the hatchet blade well waxed.
The skull serves as a paperweight
or a reminder of your next
appointment with the dentist. Buff
and rinse, the clean drill gets the last
of the dull clinging film right off.
Grin at the nurse.

                      But you know that rust
on the hatchet would be a different story.
Coating with wax will keep it away
(bone round the brain).

                      Memento mori.
But in the meantime avoid decay.

5

Transmission from the promised landscape:

to the memory of Jules Verne,
to the guiding electric prophecies:
while men forgot and turned to each other
we have been lifted up, surely,
ungainly hermits of the metal creed,
to the wilderness with our holy dependence
on the artifacts of progress.

Perhaps a future primitive generation
will worship that huge disc in the sky.
Meanwhile we shall keep the radio contact tight.

The sky is black.

   6

Small neon fires light up the mouth
of the open street, glint on teeth
of stores and pool halls. My shoes grind
on the gravel, walking in no-man's-land.
I break a spent match and flick it down.
Across town I hear a siren moan.

Downstairs to the warm bar; the jukebox
winks its signals to the bottles and back.
It bounces Janis Joplin off
the pinball crash, the juiced laugh.
I'm coddled by fusing noise here.

Above the machines, in the blank air,
is the wholeness of the corpse in orbit
between the womb and the waxed hatchet.

Advice to a Popular Hero

Slide your fedora forward. Tilt yourself
at a similar angle from the wall. Move.
The big getaway this time. The big Ford's
near rear wheel spins: a can of film.

Somewhere out on the highway you will meet
your successor. You will know him by this mark:
the right-hand thumb-skin roughened by the thread
that opens up the shifting spanner's smile.

You must pretend you haven't noticed him.
Keep your eyes low. Grab a meal. Drive away.
We have replaced you, but you've only lost
a fantasy. Stick to your real work.

Man and Law

A milk-dipped finger points to trace
words on the table. Lacking grace
to speak his words against a tune,
he hides behind the afternoon.
Fingernails and cigarettes
suffer. The lines finished, he wets
his finger again. The words run
into each other. Outside, the sun
still drinks the suburb through a straw.
Hands are still weaker than the law.

"O *triste, triste était mon âme
à cause, à cause d'une femme,*"
he writes, forgets the rest. He who
would terrify the world has to
convince himself he is not sane,
obliterates the lines again.
from the bruised throat human pride
still bubbles like the day outside.
self-imposed penances are for
those who understand the law.

So curse Verlaine with woman-kind.
A man should hide behind his mind
if anywhere. Rage. Rage. He tries,
but he can only terrorise
citizens with cups of tea
whose eyes are ordered not to see
the shame extending from his hands
back to the brain which still demands
strength against the open door
letting in sunlight like the law.

He leaves the table, walks across
to the door, breathes, knows his loss
more clearly by looking at his fists.
The shaft of golden dust persists.
The mess of milk on the table dries.
Soon the inexorable flies
will come. He steps into the yard.
The sun burns through the soft facade
of shame to uncover even more
strength than he needs to break the law.

Sydney's Drowning

Sump oil maps the cement floor;
Aladdin's tool-box treasure for the poor
lies open. Now a know-all salesman smiles.
The spanner's in the flesh. Adjust the brakes.
The end product, gloss, fairy floss
spun on a lathe. Tick off the clockwork miles.
The electro-magnetic crusher makes
tidy blocks to be sunk in rows across
the bay. The drivers are inside.

So let the harbour take you for a ride.
The foot wavers before the ferry. Pause.
Sabotage suspected. Seek out the cause.
The shattered surface tilts. See the cracks
spread down through Kirribilli. The axe
is on the block. The deckhands are too smart.
Headlines and preying hovercraft. Let terror pass
and watch the bridge sweat in the night.
Hear the chiffon-throated girl squeal with hope.
The cowboy hats are made of fibre-glass
this year. Their cords are tight.
Slim Dusty probes the communal country heart
of Luna Park with smoke between its teeth.
the water bears the weight of screaming rope.
Oil holds the answer. And the fish beneath.

Western Addition

Rectangular entrails of the open city
are plotted for spleen, pyloric valve
and other neighbourhood highlights
by the 5 McAllister bus as it crosses
Van Ness, Buchanan, Steiner, Broderick.
here, inside the various chambers,
organs and auricles of the breathing body
the music mounts, you feel your arrival;
Divisadero.
Yo son un hombre sincero.
not just at a bus-stop
but at a point of human wonder,
like the ten-year-old thin fist
in salute from a doorway,
like hollow Thunderbird eyes along Fillmore.

Last century, the city fathers had a plan,
grand as a gingerbread house,
flat as a street map,
a living plaque to progress,
a net of streets laid over hills.
But something escapes, runs down
through one corner—Visitacion Valley—,
flows past the whale of the Cow Palace
and banks up in the San Brunos;
beyond them America begins,
all that is not the City begins.

Towards Tamalpais
the bridge floats, delicate vermilion,
over the memory of Modoc families.
The mountain is softly being
a deity of the cloud-Americans.
She gives no sign.

She will always be there.
Turn quietly back to the white buildings.

Out across the Pacific the air gets crazier;
the heavy clouds troop like islands.
Fantastic trees and outriggers, blood coral,
volcanoes, meridians, *Australia Felix* unmanageable,
storm after calm, pale shells and the wreckage
of World War II Lancasters, dislocated jewellery
that the albatross presides over.

Go too far past the Avenues
and you're in the element
of Coleridge and Fletcher Christian.

Cross the Great Highway
and you're dead.

The first task is to avoid dying,
to move out beyond the fog, to move
where the air is hot and empty.

The second task is to avoid death,
to recognise and overcome
the solipsistic accretions
inside your single skull.

The vacant winds fling up
hitlerian images when you run
from the old cliche, the stumbling old
block of your father's
headmasterly morality.

When that's gone,
what've you got left to lose?
the metanoid pressure of a pose,
art for art's sake,
the racial fantasies that claim us,
crying "culture" in a chill solo:
only this, and the last seven years,
the time it took to cross the ocean.

Here in the quiet of the Panhandle,
in your denims and twenties
(both wearing thin) what have you learned
from the kids strung out along the Haight,
from *los Siete*, from the saucer of sweet graffiti
that is Hayes Valley? . . . Divisadero.
Yo son un hombre sincero.
The fierce uncomfortable art
of being honest—faith in history,
con los pobres de la tierra
love where it belongs: in action,
strength where it must be found.

California

Phil Spector made this state,
hurled it down from his god-high box
adding layers of freeway lanes
smash on smash, souped-up, laid down
like surf on Pescadero
like NOW SOUND slammed onto a disc

and it lay, bay-flat, farm-flat.
Its mountains were forgotten beyond the flat smog.

Only the round
melons olives onions grapes
grew upwards and were lifted
into the sunlight by the campesinos
who, their labour forced like fruit
from the flat earth,
twisted, sweat-scored,
drenched with DDT,
grew upwards and together, whole as a vine,
against the traditional fall of things,
against the angry put-down.

People make mountains,
ranged together in a picket line,
a simple Sierra
growing out of the trailer-camps,
the car-bodies, the disease,
and into the rich air
where the sun bursts like juice.

Sacramento: this is my body.
Take. Eat. This is my hope.

Elegy for Jenny

Few of us loved you at the end. You made
it hard. The tunes you sang to were all played
in crazy octaves no-one else could reach.
The winters you spent drinking at the beach
your fibro cabin looked down where the old
corrosion went on. Thought could never hold
it back, no more than ships could chart a course
by whisky bottles glinting their mad morse
or others' proper wisdom ease the stress
of pain and fear. Too often consciousness
obscures the lines of memory it tries
to follow. Nerves alone can ride the lies,
are capable of pity; they alone
can know the faults and scobs of every bone
and trace a vision over them. My pain
will teach me some time what there is to gain
from yours: the hot cirrhosis locked in tight.
Essentially your balance was in flight.
And when the crasis turned it led to where
the cartilage, the marrow and the hair
are laid down, muffled talk and loam and pine
complete the ceremony. In a line
five strangers standing at the grave's wet edge
face only ground-mist and the black yew hedge.
Outside, the ocean lies like a straight fact
and living minds through light-waves interact;
clothed in plastic, new transistors play
and all the dancing commerce of the bay
continues, threading winter with bright noise.
Outside your beach house, Jenny, teenage boys
in wetsuits ride the breakers in to land
where basalt has become fine silver sand.

Aubade

Mornings I feel it worst. The cold comes in
like consciousness. The mirror turns pale grey.
The razor drags its rash around my chin.
I must get myself assembled for the day.

This daily detumescence out of dream
shocks like linoleum. I can't turn back.
Now I'm fully awake my wishes seem
laid out like hectic ties along a rack.

Shivering, severed, skinned like grapefruit segments,
my brain cells jar with sunlight. It's a task
less worthwhile every day to fit the fragments
of my dislocated face into a mask.

Autumn

I Behind the Phoenix Foundry

Mallarmé's curse rides over Launceston.
Autumn sticks to the foundry yard.
This morning had the old trick in it:
the air virgin, dry,
pretending cleanliness.

What is tempting now
is the easy elision, the colour-coded sketch:
to surround the sonnet with absence
like a page.

Let the hero go spinning out into his margins.
Open the tombs.
Observe the chemistry of after-death:
nitrogen, seepage, the skilled craft
of bacteria.

The racks of angle-iron are bright
with flux. Oxygen creates
these orange flakes. Real gases
control the world. Two kids
play here, off the street, safe,
in harmony with the tough scrap.

II Fisherman

Where is the old stability?
The dinghy wobbles on the ebb.
Who will come home
past the long island?
(Eucalypts stand green.)
No-one coughs blood. This is not Valvins.

Through the heads with the tide:
one, singing at the tiller,
shirtless impresario,
burnt against the clouds?
Idle speculation.
Thank god and Dampier our swans are black.

III Against Mallarmé

This is a canny pioneer country.
The trees stay the same colour
until they're scrubbed and
trucked and chipped and sold.
The unnerving smell of the bush
has been a challenge to the genius of man
for cyclic comfort. Man,
on his own terms, wins, and gets
Pinus radiata where birds don't go.

Even while the mist of fish blood
spreads, "effulgent haze", from
the hard hope of the knife,
the fisherman knows
that one day the catch will be
something stranger even than his song.

A leaf from an imported tree
falters, then settles.

The kids are called in to the terraces.
An absence of their playing remains.

The poem, however, refuses to hang about,
will neither be caught nor rust,
is not dependent on seasons,
but is being forged
in the haul, in the furnace,
the real grave and the game.

Poems 1974–1979

Grammar

The runes and ratchets of our time
picked from the soft stone, ore
forged and formed, cog and rhyme,
base and superstructure for
the shape in which we change and grow.
Architecture: history
frozen in the *logos*, so
is language the struggle to be free.

The way men work, the relationship
between them and what they do
shapes the syntax of the age.
As the machines stick and slip,
as the suffixes accrue,
so the lines run on the page.

Jet Lag

Landing: the thick glass yawns,
flat weeds tangle a cover over
suburbs with goalposts, frail pikes
of pleasantry. Communal control-towers
on every neighbourhood hill crop out.

The statues in the lounge are shaped like chairs.
Dryness is a stale relief,
furry and racked. After the flight,
ailerons conning Urizen's arsenal
of treacherous water-forms, terminal puns
doubly fool. Vistas, through doors that lick,
onto slewing traffic present you with the past.
Come home to the colours of the future.

Take tokens: derris to stun fish,
a vorticist map, a chip of hot melt.
Then watch the man punch his greyhound in the head
as they walk past the burning shop.
Breton said it will usher you into death.

Squad

Pasted inside the blindfold
are the snapshots of despair.

Camaraderie of blank beads
reciprocally drawn, in the know,
readies the show,
steadies the fingers and my nerveless
aim: to see it through
the ritual puffs, to thank whoever will
fire my last smoke,
a spiralling request:

to see
the cut-outs of my family
pop up,

sideshow targets to collapse
into my sockets.
They will resume their rounds
in the hidden alleys of a skull.

Roulette

Five empty vodka glasses
over the shoulder, blind,
satisfy. The last of the six
squats on the table, full of oil.

Evening darkens its cylinder to metal,
a dull tumbler loaded with the odds.

It spins cold now in night.
Dancers' heels click; echoes run
without a catch throughout
the straight grey corridors
of midnight palaces.
I live in the empty chambers.

Five Trees

EXOCARPOS CUPRESSIFORMIS

The old lady used to sit with her barley-water
frightening her grandchildren's friends.
Her fat son bowled googlies at us on the driveway.
Other times we'd sit and suck the native cherries,
plan fish-traps of immense cunning, brag
of how many times we could swim across the bay.

The sound of the tennis ball hitting the black Ford
was like the gulp of air we'd taken in
when we watched them hang the man who'd shot Dad's friend.

The old lady's blotchy skin was like the photos
of the corpse in the newspaper we'd pored over.

The native cherries tasted sharp, at least.

BURSARIA SPINOSA

The box-tree straggles into the summer holidays
off-white, a drunken bride reading the telegrams
by mistake. Empty bottles, bleached form-guides
and strips of manna bark pile round its base.
Last summer the baby got tetanus after a cut
from a rusty knife she found lying here
under the box-tree. It was touch and go for a while.
What amazes me still is how she reached it
without getting scratched by the thorns. I'll clean it all up
some day.

        Meanwhile the pedicles stand to the sky,
light as lint. It's nearly New Year.

Acacia melanoxylon

When they found old Terry he'd been dead for a week.
There was no garden to speak of round his shack,
but in the front paddock stood a mighty blackwood
symmetrical and pure. Driving past,
you couldn't take your eyes off it.

                                            Blackwood,
the most beautiful of trees.

                                    It was the Rigby boys
who found him. Shook them up a bit, they said.
They buried him down in the town cemetery.
Should've put him under that blackwood, I said.

There was no glass in either of his windows.
He used to chuck his food scraps out of them
to feed the possums, rats and chooks.

Casuarina stricta

The kids of the people we bought the house from
had a cubby-house of she-oak branches
up against the back fence. Only the funnel-webs
used it for a couple of years. Then I burned it down.
Took half the fence with it, but the tree
they'd ripped the branches from remained, surrounded
by black waste. There are patterns in its bark
which modulate into the fruiting cones.

It is important not to let the patterns break down.
The past must remain personal. It's complicated enough.

So when the rusty flowers fall, covering the ash,
there will be a basis. I won't have to let
the children or the spiders back in. I can live
my past out with the tree and stand
next to it and stand on the new soil.

Myoporum insulare

The beach is asbestos. Here I will not burn.
In fact, the boobiallas and the railway line
have lost their link with light. Yesterday three bodies
were washed up, two small boys and a teenage girl,
all fully dressed, looking normal. The day before,
a young bloke in overalls. Today I'm waiting
for the score. I've chain-smoked, burying the butts
in the grey sand. The smell of the purple berries
is the smell of death now. The *Tasman Limited*
will come past in twenty minutes. When it does
I'll laugh. I haven't laughed for two days.

I would like to come here, under the boobiallas,
every day for a few hours

and watch the sea.

Clare

birth

    My favourite butcher's hands are never as bloody
    as this obstetrician's.
    My motor mechanic's overalls are always spotless.
    (He used to work in the pits at Le Mans.)
    Neither of them has much faith
    in meatless machines.

14 months

    Poised: pens   matches   smaller books
    are prey   All dead things
    The hyena, too, is always happy.

future

    You cannot take Garaudy's advice
    to "love the future".
                      So you are safe
    from expulsion.
                  I cannot say the same
    for myself.

Bag of Shit

Looking forward to the pleasure of anticipating,
you can always beat the panic
by getting in ahead.

This is the age of the cherishing gadgets.
Isolated with accoutrements
our single rooms are safe as plastic bags.

Lay a new track through the map,
the old connections, berserk loops,
for the dinning freight.

When the shit kicks
relax inside the rush.
Be warm. Sleep warm. Sleep.

Sleep cold. Kick the bag.
It's too big. It plops
on the hard floor and stinks of shit.

80° 08' 1934

> *"May was a round boulder sinking before a tide."*
> — Richard E. Byrd

Carbon monoxide like an aurora
in my veins blinding the haemoglobin
until nerve-ends are pellets
of fierce drift, June 1st:
three months on the wrong side of the sun,
my heart like the skipping engine
in the tunnel, its exhaust rimed up,
sending the blank gas round again
dizzying me down to two red candles,
one in a cracked china holder,
the other planted in its own tallow,
I have the tiny data on a shelf
in the Escape Tunnel. I have jobbed
in the substance of truth.
If they should have to come for me . . .
I am a Virginian.
I am a thin flame drawn between two voids.

Polheim

Favour walked with us,
the sixth comrade.
Death was a light secret like
Wisting's tobacco,
triumph a handy weapon
stowed in close
for quickly clubbing the dogs
according to order.
Order was easy to haul.

we whipped out victory, snapped
it to the pole
in a breeze.

The Worst Journey in the World

Head in the block of ice
his balaclava had become,
Birdie almost complained
the third day of the blizzard
with no tent. Cherry, blind even
in England, in day, "just did
what he was told". Gentle Bill
who did not trust fit sailors
had chosen them. Five weeks
of black, of pain, tea, pemmican,
biscuits, a birdnesting spree,
thumping each other's limbs for hours
to free clothing enough for rest.

Was the orgy still on in the Hut?
Who danced the Lancers with Anton?
They had peaches with syrup.
They had colours.

                        Camped high
out on the moraine under Terror
three aristocrats on a graceful
romp in Hell, life an egg balanced
on the toes of the shuffling
amateur Empire, found the tent
—a stick in the wide fury of ice—
bore it, a relic, given.

The Emperor eggs, the absurd grails,
had no embryos, were no use
for advancing ridiculous theories.

Onyx River

The river of remembering
runs where there is no ice,
where coal seams album
chronology of hot trees,
fossils and grains of pollen,
penguin bones, Devonian items.
Here the bloom of slime is a
wipe of origin again.
Bacteria shift in their thin
ritual in the tenuous soil.
An oasis of noise: stones
the sun ribs through water chatter,
melt puddles move, colour
of the first fish, of the always
sun and the lake takes
dead mountains down and, blue,
robs them with hope. *Again*
is the bludgeon of slight cells
against a continent.

Mawson Alone

This corpse, this garbage, subtly
drew my fierce love, my precious
flame gone useless, hard, white,
not even measurably
like my single fingernails
or the strong warm dogs: Gadget,
Fusilier and Jappy, Betli,
Blizzard, six in the crevasse, then
George, Johnson, Mary, Haldane,
Pavlova and Ginger; nor
like Ninnis, silent, sudden
as lancing a whitlow.
But if the hot spread of hoosh
was joy this was its negative:

so much breath spent warming
the snow, love put out on the waste
chest of Mertz, light as an albatross.

Growth

"My father he is in Australia.
He has cancer of the stomach.
There is no cure. You know that?"
Then he went on to ask me about
bank interest rates and the price of potatoes.

I thought of those tubers in the dark vaults,
earth at home red as money, of increase.

Decay enriches. The clusters feed,
nodules of capital, silent.

Pain comes for an old man round
as coins too late to spend
or save.

      Invest for life.
Bankers are good for advice.
Doctors often lie.

Melody for a Hard Summer

Only with her subjunctive eyes
she views her body's ladder
tinged with minor shade values,
ribbons it, longly, loose
under a flaccid hat. Clothes
are a lenitive up front at
the mirror. Cream and mauve
blur the immediate air.
She lapses on to a cushion,
reads Keats with a gently wet *doigt*.

A dotterel sprigs the detritus
of a tidal curve; its cap is chucked
like a red toy. From an incongruous
restaurant Monk on an endless
loop of tape breaks the anti-glare.
The right hand shivers an octave;
what falls is dry. The brittle pattern
of adventurism slides
its advance to a rattle
on path or harder grass.

There are various poisons,
some in the water, others
in humours. Mostly they are discerned
only from symptoms. Subtly
the cloud's in the lady's
mirror, from her blood and mood.
Control shed from chords flies
off, covers the bird's bank, a plan
imposed by the anarchy of
market: "Eat my freedom!"

The tinkling dilettantes of the Left
spin off in sheets, make
words at each other. Purity
is the gladwrap of politics;
compromise the mouldy sandwich.
Poke it safely. Wait for it
to turn into a lotus.
Eat it then. Revolution
is so easy. Of course we'll all
starve in the meantime. Suck ice.

Wish on its own is fatal,
is in a room, makes no music,
cannot exploit a crisis.
If you want to be a shore-bird
study the art of wading.

Underground

So who needs to dance? In the dark night club
there are mirrors, a bar glints brands all angles
like the music trilled by toes, knees.

The celibate life! Pleasures the arse
pushes are dispensible
even in a close bed.

Clingstones, the brie in its shell,
the tight scallop, all of them
are for taste, not digestion.

Nipples will never sustain
a shawled infant. Useless to shrug
covering the neck, that meaningless ampersand.

Lying and licking never did much good.
The point of the nose has been lost;
ears, eyes received little in a black world.

Scalp and elbows were superficial jokes.
Only the fingers, long
after hope went, dance in the infinite air.

Vanzetti

The charge that smashed your nerve cells apart
had too much volume for your corpse to keep.
Nothing could earth it. From your violent start
like one of Galvani's frogs against the straps
it hopped the gap to where the crowds, deep
around the Charlestown jail, around the world,
were waiting, latent, for that spark. Perhaps
the State of Massachusetts when it hurled
its bolts at you thought that you were not
in contact, would, alone, absorb the lot.

The charge they hit you with, on the other hand,
you and Niccola, was absurdly light.
Murdering payroll guards for fifteen grand
is nothing to men who wanted the big haul:
not just the money but the means; who'd fight
not cops or even judges but the force
that owned those forces, lethal capital.
Wrong in law and fact, Thayer was right, of course,
to sentence you. Bourgeois justice in this case
would have been hindrance, but it knows its place.

The heaviest charge is what you've laid on us:
to keep transmitting those raw lovely volts
until they think we're all as dangerous
as you and Sacco. Who will then be shocked?
Meanwhile we insulate, check for shorts and faults
and grope for the master switch somewhere among
the bizarre trappings of the power that knocked
your body shuddering like a prophet's tongue
that's running on and down when all is said
but nothing done yet by the woken dead.

Blade

The first hint is a gleam.
The shell of a wave could be
flattening its curl under the moon.
Then the easy slide

surprises, testing for texture,
finding it smooth, barely
noticeable till the twist
that opens. A tendon gives.

When you clean fish well
a bundle of various organs,
orange, cream, cherry-black,
falls, still compact, out.

Bolt

Massive black hyacinth
squeezed power, centuries bunched
fear over head, solitary, bald,
armed and erect with nerves
—a quiver of golf clubs—.

Whose is the sport, then,
in late summer, late in the day?
There is no *hubris* in a grown man
alone with an absurd game,
nothing to call down the gold quarrel,

the renardine slash that jags,
moreover, *over* sluggish animal.

Was it that cinders zipped
excessive light up to charge
the dry, rubbing bulbs of air?
Burn heaven with a grey key? Can you
tell just like that, quick as . . . ?

Or say: the dog is lazy, died.
Dead, judge the fox.

Song for Seychelles

I

The waves slide in onto the lee shore
gently as the drift of continents.

When the granitic plates sailed off
carrying as trophies Africa and Asia
the stiff backbone of Mahé refused, remained,
until the charming princes of the West
raped her awake, pampered her with vanilla,
cinnamon, mangos, tea, TV and taxis.

II Vallée de Mai

But through the aeons of the lonely coma
monsoons persistently brought dreams of Eden.
Before the cayman grew its legs and died
this was the garden where the deal was made:
the coco-de-mer, the woman's haunch, for life
in paradise: a fair exchange, considering
that jets now fly them back, day-tripping,
making up for lost time. It's now
400 Rupees each for the fruit of knowledge;
a boy will stamp them "paid for" at the gate.
They'd rather look for shells than good or evil.
So Eve in a string bikini squeals at crabs
while Adam hacks at a coconut. Lilith
disguised as a green lizard watches, smiles.
She's seen through the coffin lid, the snorkeller's mask,
been through the glass to wonderland and back.
She knows the pretty past and her old patience
taught her then only to love the future.

III Liberation

Fifth of June, 1977:
a line of surf slices between the red
of coral and the green of takamaka
to make a flag that cuts, shines and continues.

Coconut palms thrown at the sky like starfish
announce the sudden sunrise and embellish
its proclamation. Liberty and justice
are heavy words. Pirates and colonists
threw them overboard, ran light for home.
But the reef held them captive; the sun hit
through the pale shallows; they were there for the taking.
Ashore they stand like the rock at L'Union.

The last bearded corsair's in port in Europe;
he's left his doubloons buried in the sky.
Pieces of sweat glint, fish-scales in the sun.
That will be capital enough to build
a miracle. Where fish and foxes fly
ideals can leap into reality.

from *The Atlas* (1982)

I

Fear didn't fly back with Kilroy
after the Battle of Brisbane.
Fear wasn't burnt out of man
at Hiroshima. Nor was it shipped
with the bullion to Batavia.

Hope had come marching out of Changi.
Hope was a nurse with Rita Hayworth hair
and a Silent Knight. In town, it was
a union card, a Commission weatherboard.

Here, in the slick under the bowsers,
red dust and sun on the fumes
flavoured the fourpenny cordials.
Hope was fear. Bushfires could change
the colour of hills. Teachers and farmers
misread peace. Fear was only
hope on the black market. Here
the red soil and the subtle seasons
were the inscrutable enemy;
farmer, teacher, butter-factory manager,
you wrestled heifers or the deficiencies
of fat girls with dull brown eyes.

It was at the black
edge of the market,
it was in the shed with
the rifle and shotgun,
in the bank manager's
voice and the headlines,
that the contradictions
impinged out here.

Then they were clear as the sudden horn
of Colonel Kelly's jeep at midnight.

Fear at the coal-face:
every track and tread
gripping more than frosty
overburden: the shoulders
of the five-year-old in the back
of the narrow new Ford Prefect
catching the edge of excitement
in his father's voice as he and
the local black-marketeer
praised Chifley at the dusty
side of a country road.

II

This, then, was the city.
I would learn to cope, slowly,

nursed in the sedulous old stone
mapped with mosses,

a huge cottage
nestled at the top dizzy

edge of its own stone's quarry, crazy
and soothing.

Upstairs lived the old woman
they said. Below

the quarry: the stone warehouses,
the harbour soft with yachts.

The narrow bakery
filled the lane air at night;

dully from the pubs and wharves thuds
of car-doors, cargo;

traffic was the unknown, the big
intersection was a cross for a country kid

in Battery Point, enclosed
by trucks and the bedless Derwent

where water slowly became alluvial silt,
thicker and warmer, down

to the earth's muddy core. Here, though,
was a village; the ways of strange adults

worked for me: a circle to
charm and cocker.

Each morning Dad would work
the Prefect across town

and out into where a thousand children
were tumbling, new,

the berry-orchard slopes
from thin houses.

I would stay.
The world of the old garden

rose around me. There were
cousins of some strange remove

to play with. They knew
about the city.

They went to a school that had uniforms,
carried books across the road.

One of them rode a bike in the streets.
They told me about the old woman.

My filter, they made the secrets
I learned from them

pure as the water where
the chop of the river lapped sun.

Quarry-edged blocks
of knowledge lodged

in my mind. I did not know.
The buildings were too hard.

The old woman perched
at the top of her house

was its capital.
Cousins flowed round her.

Messages like sails
kept her. She never came downstairs.

She must have smelled
the same bread, watched the ferries.

The stone had loved her
to crumbling.

   III

Index, middle and ring
fitted the mountain just across
the river. Across the river
meant, first, a link, wonder.
There, from the kitchen window
to the farms like knuckle-wrinkles,
flat and wide, water. Later,
a separation, wondering at.

. . . spoke of "Melbourne", of "overseas",
I was confused. Where were the castles,
the double-decker buses, the Taj Mahal,
the MCG? was that Dick Whittington's road
at the base of the mountain? What was beyond?
Apart from the visible connection
with the three-fingertip mountain
I made none. There were
two worlds.

Then Alfred arrived in the street,
seven with an old man's head
and an old man's name. It was wrong.

He was a nazi, a refugee,
dirty, couldn't play cricket.
Alfred, scrubbed and slavic,
and his grandmother with no voice
for English, but dark words
under her shawl linking
the young suburb with unclear
reverberations of old
fears in other places.

Even across the water there was
no Treblinka, Lidice, Hoess.
Later the atlas opened out
one world on a double page.

V

Emblems set high: a bell, a ram's skull,
to force necks into attention, to force
thought. The men who placed them there knew
the first law of propaganda: commitment
follows the expenditure of effort.

The bell, carved in relief from stone
above a shop-front: *Thos Bell & Sons*
was more than a monumental pun.
The original *Thos* was a convict, Thomas Higg,
brassmonger's lad sent out for stealing a bell.
In 1814 on a gang clearing scrub for a farm
out Lewisham way, and "being troubled by blacks"
he devised a scheme for clearing them as well.

A bell was hung on a pole in a cleared patch.
A few times a day someone would ring it. At dusk
they'd go back the half mile or so to camp.
Soon one bolder native came and tried it,
went back, delighted with the sound, then more
the next night, ringing, laughing at the toy.
The third night the four guards stayed,
bagged three in the dark. From then for years
throughout the area out-parties all took bells.

Freed as reward Higg took up a new name
and after some industrious years' employ
saved enough to set up in business,
his life's token as shop sign to prosper under.
140 years on, the school books
have him as hero. His great great
grandson changed his name to Smith.

The skull, on the other hand, was placed
on the crossbar of a hydro pole
by linesmen, a trophy from
a rather more subtle conflict.

This is "sheep country", pockets of plain
and gorsed escarpments, high to wind
snow and sun. Dumb mutton
turns its harsh elements to fleece
and blown dags. The stupid ram
tups and butts, dies in drought
or spring snow. Animal without
country or cunning, the blind invader
suffers victory, adapts defeat.

This was wallaby country. English grass
has superfined it. Pence a pound
is the measure of colonial success.
The chinless grazier humps the old Merc to town;
Bradford and Osaka nod; their argonauts
return. Everyone's happy. The thaw
runs off to nothing. New growth
browns again under a galvanised sky.

So the skull nailed up says
like a shilling against the sun
"This is man country. Fuck ewe."

Every summer we would drive
through the Midlands, leaving the old port
to stew in its stone. Insulated
from the hills of crows we would speed
through country yellow as a road map
to the coast. Devonport, grandfather's pub
was a haven from history. Whoever made
this town did not believe in emblems,
nailed nothing to lintels. Buildings
themselves embodied the spirit of the time:
1912, built for a future
of peace, dead before the paint
could enter history too. Surface
town, coastal, facing the future
with a blank sea gaze; perfect
facades to hide behind for a holiday
of death, geometrically ornate,
this was as good a place as any
to claim the shallowest family roots.

INTERLUDE

The boy running through scrub
down the morphine cliff, upright,
amazing, to the mangroves,
will not be slowed down by mud,
will, in fact, put on speed:
a crab among oysters, a dream
skidding, an escapee.

Bracken impedes the flailing
screws but the real obstacle
is their unfamiliarity
with fear and the sheer drugs
which the mind manufactures.
The skull fed by blood is a wall
unscaleable. They are brave.

The kid is ignorant.
He dances across the surface
of the bay. Memory lights
his way. It rains. He is scared
and sobs. His mind is destroyed
by the dark but his nerves
are as sure as blades and as blind.

One of the warders is armed
but he wouldn't dream of shooting.
The boy has no record of violence.
He's got kids that age himself,
loves the little crims in a way.
They call off the search at 2,
go back and write a report.

The boy dreams of shooting; all night
under an upturned boat
adrenalin pumps his sleep
with images of defiance.
The next day they don't come
for him. He squats and looks
across the bay at the walls.

A week goes by. He has coped,
found berries, fished even.
There are no shacks on the island.
He knows they have binoculars.
After a month they come.
He goes back happily.
There are no questions, no hole.

The next day he makes a shiv,
sticks the fatherly screw,
bolts, heads for town this time,
steals a gun and ammo, holes up
in the Cross, paranoid for days.
Finally, gets an education
and is never heard of again.

VII

The pale crags:
it is climbimg
they summon to.
Below, boobiallas
and bracken, rooted
soft in old loam.
The way spotted with
lichen, up. There,

the odd gull
closes a circle,
a lid on top
of a holiday.

There is always ambiguity
in limits, in holidays in particular
and in the interpretation of history.

The surface of the turquoise world
is goggle glass. The salmon idyll
ends and begins with a glint
no less slippery. Adamant,
a diamond, scales of sun
are points of flint to nourish pain.
a thin bone of light lodges
in the eye of a slim boy, wet as blood.

In Budapest there is wriggling.
The ambiguous tanks are an ocean,
a heaving aquarium brown
with weed, studded with delicate
starfish, life-giving predators.
Unlike the smaller organisms
that spit toxicity from the grit
and dart like snipers, the starfish
cling to a stolid love and do not move.

The ecological paradox, work and play:
kids like crabs lug .22s, chew on the stocks
for the CIA; the tide-pool foams
in a sudden rush, settles like an eye.

The water is so clear a shadow
disturbs the programmed ribs of sand
a fathom under. A school will choose
collectively which way to twist.
The shadow of Mindszenty hangs from the rock
of the West. The cormorant's beak threatens
a fascist wedge towards the sea-floor steppes.

Here is a beach to scuttle to, bewildered.
Here the boy can break the crust of sand
and smooth a towel and look at the crags.
Here is a place to shiver dry.

The dangerous sunlight slides like skin,
spreads into five gold tapered radii
clinging to the creamy peaks.
There is no fear in climbing, so no hurt.
The injuries are only in the mind.

   XIII

Bluffed by daylight, bundled
from bed out to the farm kitchen,
sat with the four strong sons
square at the pine table slabbed
with ham, spuds and tea in huge mugs,
I feel my town years, thin
and crustless, refined away
from rhythm. The sun's heat
is overbalance. Cold muscles
tug my bones to it through the
waiting air over the large yard.

In the creek down by the front gate
a platypus lives under a willow-green
ledge, merged in the cool by day.

Land, the possession of land,
puts Uncle Cal in the driver's seat
of the Massey-Ferguson. He moves
towards the sun as slowly as a noble,
overturning the plants in steady rows,
dispensing bags at measured intervals.

My shoes, old but unsuitable,
fill with the sun-red soil
for three hours. Then we sit,
the lads joking with cream-cake
in the shade of the tractor.

The platypus sleeps under the willows.

Shaking down the bags as they fill
with spuds and sun gets harder.
The sky is now royal with heat.
the dirt claims me more every time
I straighten up. The tractor makes smooth
curves at the end of each row, returns
relentless but itself driven.
The order is fixed in levels, down from
the divine element to the kids
from the next farm spotting chats for pence
like gulls at the far end of the paddock.

In its own colours, its own scheme,
the queer wet mammal is outside this.

By dusk the bags are squatting
like castles. We douse and change,
eat enormously. The eldest cousin
cons the car. We cruise out.
At the gate we shine the flash
under the willow. The platypus
grins with its riggish beak.

On the road we do wheelies, play chicken,
drag all-comers, tailgate on high-beam.
Bottles, still in their paper bags,
are handed round; you never get
past the froth. Crash Craddock
and Fabian from the local station
ride with us, urge us on.
Someone knows some girls
whose parents have gone out for the night.
There we sit around on beds,
read comics, pair off. As I trace
the warm new map of a body,
puckered areola, tiny thigh-down,
my lips protrude, calloused, to a bill,
my fingers are constrained by their webs.

XIV

Friday afternoon: assembly, then *Pro Archia*;
the *optimates*' ethics rattle down
the corridor.
Frank Richard Cowell has a Civil Service face.
His spine is tatty.
Bradley's Arnold, smug and fat,
has all the answers.
Old Tully that preposterous obnoxious turd

sold his voice and we're still paying.
Saxa et solitudines voci respondent: like buggery!
Tell that to the geology master.
Christ how poor Archias must have winced.
cantu flectuntur. It's a pity
there weren't a few *bestiae immanes*
in the Forum that day
to chew on you like a pea.
I am a rock and a solitary place.
I am seventeen
and you are a useful thing for me.

Lentulus didn't live to hear this one.
Cethegus was strangled in his cell.
Gabinius and Statilius, too,
choked on your *animus popularis*.

They got Lumumba the same way.
The CIA should hire a lawyer
to defend a second-rate poet this year.
But they don't have your tongue, your rolling
ut and *ac* and *hoc* and *sed*,
dry chick-peas in a vault.
The rhetoric's gone.
Our headmaster lacks style, but then
two thousand years is a long time.

He looks like *Bradley's*, green, thick,
oil for teenage troubles.
I hit him in the stomch once,
an "accident", no more satisfying
than slamming the book when your pronouns get out of hand
in *Oratio Obliqua*. He's an old
Opus Dei boy from way back;
I've checked him out.

The Latin master's skinny in the head
like Cowell: another mick
(they're every-fuckin-where)
but liberal, more brains than
these protestant kids who work hard,
giggle when they make a mistake
and think their cunts are for pissing out of.
I've given up making mistakes.
Being perfect's the only worthwhile pose.

"A Rockefeller Research Fellowship
in the Social Sciences", de Gaulle,
the CMG. Of course he'd say
"Catiline and his motley gang
were wiped out" just like that.
Lumumba got it from someone with
as nice a sense of the colloquial,
or probably better; "motley" betrays
the Roan and Kings background, the easy
acceptance of due, of the *mos maiorum*.

Stuck with this motley gang
I'll take the worst, the hired tongue,
for close companion or the afternoon
would be unbearable. Come on, you shit,
I'll romp my wits through your grammar,
test my knowledge with your Greek echoes,
forget the crap and train my ear for style
with your chiasmus and your quantities.

Interlude

By the Greystone bed, mock-cowboy hat in hand,
shuffling a homage to the poet, to the poetry,
the trapeze artist acknowledges his sawdust base.
Blind eyes and rhinestones meet, the skyway shoots
with song that will not rot, galactic pulse
the twirling hat, the whirling dust combine to will.

> *All day they pump me with paralysis and pain.*
> *They have taken the coursing from my voice, the limp*
> *and stuttering blood is pricked with weird additives.*
> *Curlylocks, Curlylocks, wilt thou be mine?*
> *Mine like the harvest, twisted by bitter wind*
> *out of the blight, hot sweat composting battered roots*
> *spiked with grit, wormed with words, ours, song!*
> *Zither-man, slimmer-man, nor yet feed the swine.*

Yours were the lessons, silent teacher, crafty singer.
Along ten thousand years I learnt by heart in the dark
glory road signposts, learnt to write the hurricanes,
to read the cards, and when I fly from this, our first
meeting, it will be in a machine made by your wit, your work.
I can't make prose to you but I will live our song.

XVI

The stage is the world.
He trissed in lilac, flourishing
a Mannlicher-Carcano 91/38,
hideous to the pit, but from the gods
lisping grace against the pseudo-
Beardsley backdrop. This is style:
derivative from decadence, treading
a step beyond tatty death, turning
entropy on its head. Art has survived
art-for-art's-sake, flaunts its victory
for the sake of art: a performance.

The boy in the lighting box
is on his second bottle of vodka.
The spot wanders. The background changes
slowly from pastels through fiery orange
until its red is insistent, out of proportion
to the language of the play. As for the shot
(or shots), reports conflict. The audience,
questioned in the foyer, was unanimous:
the actor's lips were fuller than is healthy
as if they carried too much blood.
His face otherwise was a cadaver's.
Was this just a matter of make-up?
Those who knew him offstage gave differing answers.
He had disappeared at the instant of blackout.

The victim's brunette widow, meanwhile,
wears his blood becomingly for the TV cameras.
The Secret Service men are grimly handsome.

XIX

Across the playground the cadets
wheel and halt, snap their limbs
in their ridiculous webbing, neat
in khaki, rationalised, an even unit.

The repetition of simple drills works
better than deduction, trains the spirit
to respond correctly, the fingers and mouth
to respond without interference.

Today we have Webb's "The Mountains."
See how the verbs work like veins.

Outside, the noun
governs the sentence like a brigadier,
its attribute strapped to it.
"National defence", "Communist expansion"
repeated, repeated, educate us all.

I go on teaching. Bill White would, too,
but for a few months, a few marbles
that rolled in a hollow barrel,
sentences in a politician's mouth.

Would they learn, Ricky and Craig,
Raelene, Debbie, would they come to understand
from the instant of contradiction
how the perversion of language turns
teacher to murderer, or how
resistance bears out their lessons?

The village school at Man Quang
was examined last year by Skyraiders.
Thirty-four kids and their teacher
failed completely. They hadn't understood
the logical language of pacification.
Johnson's curriculum had left them for dead.

Beyond the question of syntax
is the problem of form on the larger scale.
The novel for compassion? Late at night
after marking I'd disintegrate.
The final effect was too far
from the dialectic of vowels and grammar
where love begins. I learnt this from Dylan.

Language and love: the occupational
harmonies. Active use for social ends
will liberate. We drill structures
individually and in rough chorus.
Where are we heading in English and French?

Diggers for dividends. Local capital
demands justice, the undeniable noun.
Its cut won't heal. Fairhall's glee
was justified; surplus liquidity
was mopped up with bandages.

Stand easy, cadets. The propositions
of public discourse will ensure a market
for your skills and your obedience.

Poems 1980–1989

Left

The subtle shift of blur to tune:
don't want to fight it; slide. Don't want.
Relax back into consciousness.
Hold the melodic line but not too tight.

Pain slips back like a companion.
Here is the clear music. Now it has a beat.
It is piped through me from the
pumping of a used swab
more vital than any organ,
even des Esseintes'.
While I pun I live—a brave facetiousness.
But spare me the lyric.

All art constantly aspires to this condition
and surgery, however negligent,
is against nature, too.
Decadence is a lot of rot.

Fluid

A lung full of ice
will stake you out.
The lucid blue
stalactites
drip through.

Who are they who impend?
What qualifications have they
put behind brilliant glass
flat on white rectangular walls?
Where?
How tall are they?

You don't want answers, y'know.
The questions hover softly
and will not stab yet.
"Nurse, is this tube
genuine plastic?"

Low Tide, North Esk

> *"Teach your children well."*
> — GRAHAM NASH

Yeah, it was simple then. You "got your shit
together", split from bad scenes and saved the world
by growing your own (dope, hair or vegies),
teaching, trout-fishing. The future was a river.

Cross the Charles Street bridge today. Look down.
Who's getting whose together now? Who's getting split?
No more hexagrams. No more I Ching.
The kids we taught then are all unemployed
again, like '29. Decades of mud
slope into Invermay.

                      Up on Barrow
the bald and glittering rocks like skulls and knees
in the Ukraine, sliced by spades of frost
(Well, genocide . . . there's something we know about.)
clarify our beginnings. Sharp and white
the crystal cuts itself to whorls, breaks, grows,
comes down past abattoirs and English willows.

The swamp squeezed down by capital, the weight
of floods and memories of floods, still throws
up the odd swamp fox, that silver greyhound, hope,
lair, cadre, single mum, full-forward.
Under the fog the simple river slides
round the silos to where our ship comes in.

Brady's Lookout

> "*La propriété c'est le vol*"
> — PROUDHON

It is a romance that gallant Matt stood here,
a fiction (not a fantasy; that awaits you
over the hill in weirdest Grindelwald).
Logic and history place him further south,
where the smell of wet sheep and capital still hangs
over the Hobart road,
where the burger and souvenir shops are as tacky
as those bark "inns": the *Royal Oak*
where Matt posted his reward for Arthur's head
and the *Woolpack* where he coated the door with Kenton's.

And where are they now, the Gunns, the Taylors,
Effingham Lawrences?
And where are all the clowns of Arthur's circus
got up like ringmasters, red targets in the bush?
Still where they were. Only the costumes change.
The power remains. The Western Tiers
are no Sierra Maestra, not even "romantic scenery".

This is "romantic scenery": "Windermere",
as if it were a lake, not a poisoned river
—another fiction, another romance—:
a cutesie church, an olde worlde pub,
the bourgeoisie playing at being sailors.
But it's a good place to keep a lookout for
what is constant, history that survives.
The coaches still bring people to be robbed.
Lies and betrayal are still our true estate.
The pretty prison keeps us in.

The ladies made a cornucopia of Matt's cell
because he never raped and only killed
redcoats and turncoats. He was so fastidious
he baulked at sharing a coach and gibbet with
Jeffries, who was sick enough to spill a baby's
brains against a gum-tree,
who raped people and then ate them.
But even he was not a revolutionary,
just a progenitor of mainstream Tassie culture,
as Matt was of its politics:
making a virtue of impotence,
conning posterity with a flash image.
What hope for an island when even its bushrangers
had no solidarity?

I'll stand here by the tourist coach,
just another wimp who quotes Proudhon
and laments that guerrilla bands have been
romanticised to impotence again.

Macquarie House

> "And the lord commended the unjust steward"
> — Luke 16:8

You are what you preserve. Generations
of CWA Vacola greengages testify:
a warehouse on every shelf to defy nature,
to soften stone-grey winters, to disburse
everyday exotica at the cold tail-end of a meal.

At the cold tail-end of an empire
household virtues thrived. Accounts were kept.
Narrow, barred windows guarded commodities
stored and recorded like convicts. Set here square
between the bleak plains and the trading ships,

the entrepot has now become a shrine
not to the husbandry of flocks, not to the shearing,
but to the fleecing, to the false manifest
and not the cargo, to the saving of skins.
The town's foundations, theft and thrift, survive.

Today they label history, lock it up
and dole it out. The surplus value
slips through the fog where the estuary
waits, long as a leech. Inventories,
waybills, receipts are shuffled with legerdemain.

This is a town for stewards and accountants:
Room at the top, over the top and away.
Suck what you can. Fatten and fall softly.
The plums plop syrupy from the jar. There's plenty
more where that came from, and as sweet.

Reds

for SPH

Autumn again: our hopes are melting down.
The weather turns Orcadian. You paint
in wind and watercolours, tidal forms,
the art of exile. This has always been
an island of artists-not-quite-in-residence.
Teachers are exiles. Our message bobs across
a sea to fellow-humans who resist,
know us as alien, cannot trust our fierce
enthusiasms. Old affirmatives,
cheerful as leaves, no stronger, fall, still bright.

Our colleague's dying where the hospital
looks out on rusty trees and murrey rain.
That culture's dying, too, 's a rumour we've
dismissed for decades. Our class enemies,
authoritative as surgeons, just can't wait
to excise vigorous tissue. Only, now,
April and May, I feel their victory,
who have been both doctors and disease.
This is the season for being patient while
malignant cells are breeding at the core.

But let's apply old remedies, fight the flames
of burning books with scarlet fire brigades,
rage red against the danger signs. Our health
is stronger than self-pity. We must build.
A century of scientific love
built Chernobyl. The cancer spreads. What next?

Surely some random active particle
will lodge where it can work a rational,
materialist miracle. After Winter, Spring.
Artists were always mutants. Working class
kids will baulk at Kulchur, will create
their own responses. Love and hope lie deep.
A sixteen-year-old I'd almost given up on
writes a superb poem — on suicide.

Bane

It was too bright, presaging
the violent colours grabbing
the colon: green and scarlet,
white, yellow, cruel as coral.

Earth in the mouth, stretched
clay-dry after puddling,
caked, catching at the back, is
catting back into the cup,

leaving the shivers to heave
down into fluttering slivers
of sweat outside. Inside
is the taste all the way back down.

It is as if wind loosened
old wire, old windows, then growled
through, slamming out shouts,
but it is only jaws, voice.

Eyes, addled, tumble back
to see the richly-venomed brain.
Tongue, even more limber, leaps
like a rat, deserter and cause.

Tight

Minimal as silk, a single fine
reminder of the soft opulent cravat
that flowed there like too much cabernet a while,

a life ago, mars the exquisite form.
Charm remains, and certainty at last:
no tremor in the pale immaculate hands,

the ring-finger only naked. What loss
is meant? Where is the knot for remembering
delight and slight danger? Sweet Thuggee!

To Ashes

In the red vacuum, inside the roar,
witless, wondering, under the vermilion
spires where the slick black gale whips,
a struggle of grim battlers slogs on.

What's the use of such pure courage?
with no aim, no record, why keep flailing
at violent logs or fences?
You won't get out. No-one will know.

But the orgy of mateship builds its own rhythms up
past work, pain, sharing, till there's enough
clear ferocity to answer the fire, till you're

in the top tank like a lobster,
in the swept-over hollow like charred pork,
or gaunt bone-angles like the Anzac trees.

On/Against the Wall

Every five years I come to Sydney,
ride the Liverpool line to check how
the graffiti is degenerating in content
but improving in visual impact.

I no longer believe that the comforting
uncomfortable slogans will network out
lke strategic intervention, allowing communities
to access developmental advocacy, even with
agenda parasitism or the Zanetti Principle.

No-one at the CCDU can help me
understand why this is so, or why
that huge patch of canna lilies between
Sefton and Chester Hill continues to intrude
on the negation of Australian Nature Poetry.
The nearby spraycanned words are "UNIQUE / MENACE".

Meanwhile Trudy of Warwick Farm is
greatly and publicly loved. Am I
missing the point? Warwick Fairfax
on the box last night stepped out
of his limo of holy love into the true
flash of fact. Beatific, his countenance
open and aerial as a bookstore that stocks Derrida,
he said nothing. In the decorated carriage
I remember this and I remember that
the Roman Empire tried to keep ASIANS OUT.

The death of language leaves from all platforms.

Launching, By George

I don't hold a man's past against him
or behind his back like a shy posy
about to be offered to the secretary
whose cleavage has convinced her boss he's in love
enough to remember her birthday and to forget
the last episode of *Highway to Heaven*,
when the bright kids got a free lunch,
as which, of course, there's no such
luck. A free man, now, that's a racing
identity of a different colour,
like a wet land rights T-shirt competition
won by an androgynous plumber from Heckenberg
who's having trouble keeping up the payments
on the only white Porsche in the whole of the Valley.
How do you define "making it in the big time"?
Being able to twist the arm of someone
who looks affably from the front page of the SMH
as if at a future when books will be beaten?

Petty Sessions

From high walls of the court house corridor
dead Burburys and Bisdees look down
on mottled lino and a kid in wet sneakers,
eighteen and on the dole, who doesn't bother
with the tiny democratic heater sharing
its useless efforts on a June morning.

$60 and one demerit point,
at twenty bucks a cheque.
"I know I done a silly thing",
swerved over the white line
to crush a milk carton . . .
"M'lord" instead of "Your Worship."

The influence of telly? No, no Rumpoles
in this bailiwick. More likely it's
the generations of deference brought back
to the mind and forelock. Thick blood tugs
hard on this frosty plateau, and those framed
visages of men who know their place

still know their places, "Woodbury House",
"Tedworth" and "Lemon Springs", and know
more than the city lawyers. The beak's
not local, though. Six weeks to pay.
Swerved over the line, but safely back in place
soon enough, no danger to others.

No danger of anything spreading
like gorse or rabbits, no threat,
soon back in place, the sneakers soon
back on the midday frost and no harm done;
at least no greater harm than when
his ancestors were flogged or dobbed to survive,

or when the only dole his grandfather knew
was at a Bisdee's kitchen door
or on a Burbury's far paddock
at midnight with a quick knife.
The portraits do not smile, even to know
that milk cartons are less likely to be crushed.

Songs of the Protest Era

(title of an album advertised on TV)

That would have been somewhere
between the Twist and the Frug.
You know, there are people today
who can still do the Twist,
even the Charleston, but it's a pity
that Arthur Murray's black
silhouetted soles never set out
clear instructions for the Protest
or the Frug.

The Napalm was popular then, too.
Nixon sold better than Chubby Checker
—records and tapes—and do you remember
that dance we used to do to something by
Creighton Abrams, "They're Playing Song My"?
The melody escapes me but the beat's still there
and the steps would soon come back, but I'm not so sure
about those zany dance crazes that swept the campuses
like Kent State.

from *The Streets Aren't for Dreamers* (1995)

The Cull

Don't they know it's going on already?
Where do they live? Where do their kids live?
São Paolo, Flinders Street Station, Dagenham:
you don't need to stay at school to learn that kind
of geography. Same planet, same street.
My koori mate Shane's got a brother in Robinvale.
You don't know what happens there? Get real!

Cops and Wormald guards are just the tip,
methodical, uniformed, doing their job.
The real bulk's deeper, where the ice-white shirts
of management trainees are medalled
only with pen clips over the heart
from nine to five, but after dark . . .

How much shit does it take to fill
a four-wheel drive? How much
self-righteousness need squeeze into one
trigger finger? Do they think
beef-faced Old Grammarians can play
football forever, not want new sport?

The light at the end of the tunnel
is mounted on roo bars and it burns
like a tyre necklace or a church barbecue.

"It couldn't happen here" say the newspapers
inside my shirt and pants against the wind
round the back of the Frosto plant.

A Landcruiser's headlights switch the mesh fence on.

Rat's Song

This is a great town.
We got the Post Office steps
where we hang out
and sometimes talk about things.
We got the car park
where you can score what you need.
It could be better . . .

      if it weren't for the board room voodoo charts
      and the flash-tied bum-boys vomiting "Sell!"
      into carphones, if it weren't for the smiles
      of greased and grateful consultants when
      a nod on the shuttle flight's as good as a drink
      at the island bar in the chairman's pool;

      if it weren't for the heaven of merchant banks
      where the Zegna'd angels bray their praise
      from the BRW hymnal, then
      this town might seem a bit less like hell;

. . . if we had Timezone
and indoor cricket and jobs.
But it's a great town.
The cops don't hassle you much.
We got a milk bar
with a jukebox and all.

Stage Dive

Not always living by proxy, nor re-living
the clip of edited glamour thrash,
the fantasy death gig safe as the States,
no, sometimes, having so heavy a need to fly
on a lead break of my own, to assert
more than dreary frenzy can: noise pure beyond sound,
a tattoo sharper than art or pain,
I make and am still and private.

Anyone can jump from the top of an amp
into a crowd. Faith in the music, in the stance,
is a bungy rope. You might as well
sit in the mall or round a bong.
You might as well muttter, "The world's fucked"
to your mates who know that's not news.

"Despair" is no more to the point
than "the devil." When the metal
gets to be more than metaphor
it's style driven all the way
till it fuses with reality.

Like when Jason's head banged back
that night we were just having a few beers
no smart-arse video director
put the clotted pink crap
on my Anthrax T-shirt.

Now I mime to the tape of his suicide
but with feeling; the memory of his sudden weight
in my arms is the bass line to a track
I'll cut one day. When I dive
it will be through all this shit and on forever.

Roadkill

The paws for jewellery, the skins
not big enough for clothes without a lot
of sewing, but good
for market kitsch.

Don't knock technology's overkill;
it hunts as byproduct. We gather,
living off and on the road,
subsistence driving.

Just as the birds have a caste system
so we clean carrion, denying ants
all but smears in the sun
red as our hands.

Your world needs our enterprise
as much as we need your crass diesel speed.
There are untouchable
hordes of us.

Advice

Always look at their eyes. It weakens them
and brings slow thoughts they can't afford.
You get to know the best marks from eyes,
to avoid the mad, the scared, the smart.
Eyes hard as money are good for a challenge;
just don't expect to win every time.
Those softened by grog, TV or work
or flashing with outreach charity are best
for a touch, a con, an easy ride.

Diversify. If you get too hooked
on one line you'll end up being pinched.
Giving head to gents in Princes Square,
the five-finger discount at the bottle shop,
dealing, of course, running a couple of sorts:
there's plenty of games to win at; just don't get
too big for your Docs. And know your place.

The suburbs in daylight are a waste. Cruise there
for odd jobs or a raffle scam or casing
and they hit the phone. The white Commodore
snaps into the crescent like a pet to heel.
People who live in houses must be sick.
They say bricks and electricity give you cancer,
but it's their minds are worse: Neighbourhood Whatchacallit,
paranoia, there's enough of that in squats.
Don't mess with the kind that prunes and sweeps.

Above all, be always on the move
but always, at the centre, still.

Words for K

So now he rapes my brain by saying "sorry"
and I bury my hair in cold sand,
swim naked in the winter ocean,
climb high to hell's ice.

Sixteen years of Daddy
bursting through clouds of brimstone dust
from the family bible, the chapel organ pumping
at my blood, at my baby innards, Mum's eyes
like vicious prayers, the circle closed
as a country congregation.

I was seventeen
when I first dared look in a mirror.
I still sleep on my stomach
in case Satan through the floorboard cracks
takes me by surprise again
to make me his favourite daughter.

And folders, drawers, rooms, mountains
won't hold all my words, my formulae,
my poems. There's no climate
the sane and faithful live in
that my statistics can describe.

Hold me but don't touch me.

Bouncer

You're here for fun? Have fun.
You're here for trouble? I'm a wall.

In there is a wall of sound, built
by the crazy masons of Spector's guild.
Between us it's safe as a hilltop city.
Mirror balls fill your drinks with gew-gaws.
Colour and commerce flash. Sweat dances
across the rainbow, zydeco to house.

I face the street, a black plain
random with calls, tracer tail-lights,
knots of pain, cold marauders.

Past my trim gut the believers
in their best market gear
file in like villagers.

Escort

Bucking with fake joy I syphon
your pride and let it soften
in the lather of our bargain.
You were the hard man, the men,
all my uncles, landlord
of every clammy flat. Now
I'm getting the rent easy
as moaning. More slippery
than any fancy drink and with
a twist, I've knocked you out
for all your jabbing. Sport
you would call it, but what's
in my purse is the price
of admission. Blind spectator,
you had thought you were winning.
Smile your limp thanks and dream
of another tough day.
When I walk to the cab rank
clad in my skirt my stiletto
heels will be rigid but the night
will ooze, fluid, around me.

Busking

Outside Myer, outside the bank,
trying to crack the silence of cold wind,

give 'em Diamond, give 'em MOR.
No-one can think and shop at the same time.

Three days a week makes food and dope
and a place to write the songs they'll never hear

about them, what they did to old Liam
with his uke and squeezebox down the Mall:

fifties folk hero, contracts, fans, all the best clubs,
now the booze and I are out to beat him.

Or what they do to each other: "The Ballad of
the Great Sale Day Disaster", "Ode to

the Plain Clothes Cop". I could give 'em
enough social comment to fill a car park.

And love songs, too, not this cute slop
but riffs and words torn from the live guts,

that flay the throat in passing, tunes as chunks
of fire and flames of skin to drench the air

with sex and pain, make them feel their need
to die now or live as flesh forever.

You can't be a star unless you are a sun
of stinking gases, uninhabitable.

I'll make it. Meanwhile, the last toddler's
been dragged from the toyshop to the car seat.

Time to pack up. As I go past old Liam
I'll drop a couple of bucks in his uke case.

Arriving in Devonport

Driving into a smashed-bottle sunset,
tape-deck spilling k d like blood and honey
into a pit, I know just how the next town waits.

Oil tanks patrol the river bank where the bridge reaches,
tentative, into the back-lit heart, a syringe of hope.
I'm sliding with the music through the streets.

I know the pubs will smell of guns, divorce,
dealerships and bigotry: too flat, too shallow
for any despair deeper than talk-back summons.

No matter how smartly plate-glass fashion slices
the hum of truth from the drum of lust for distance
hope doesn't empty showrooms or fill freezer-packs.

This town knows that. I park, cut the music
with the motor. In the river local wisdom slaps
the hull of the ferry to the anxious world.

Bear

When they put that play on
down at the community centre
I was a bear. I scared the first three rows
of welfare workers silly.

Mostly when I roar it's not an act,
more of a drama. The worst thing
is not being able to tell them,
clearly, to shut up.

Not drunk, not stupid, only
angry: I won't get in that bus
with SPASTIC painted on it;
I am grizzly with pride,

polar with disdain. In the street
I lumber, shamble, but in
the straight line of the hunt.
I am not cuddly.

from *Taking Queen Victoria to Inveresk*
(1997)

Comrade Revenant

Ghosts, for good Marxists, should be no more
than metaphors, but in the shell annexe
it's hard to keep faith with historical
materialism, 'cause Tommy Jones
still walks, his voice is still
like a file on iron, grinding a few bob a week
extra out of the TGR for the blokes.

They've paved a plaza where the flatbed trucks
were Party platforms. Concrete and steel
won't last as long as principles
or grudges. The NUR will still be scabs
when the last apprentice has wheezed and croaked
the last oral history tape to CD-ROM.

At knock-off time a spectral cop
holds up the traffic on Invermay Road
as the insubstantial hundreds wheel immaterial bikes
out the gates and pedal off
into the history that Tommy taught them
was their comrade.

The Last Muster of the Aborigines at Risdon

An English park, the picturesque safely beyond
the river, welcomes home the hunt.
Familiar trees curve to embrace
members of a family who have been
easy on their land for generations
and easy with each other's grace.

So much is given, tacit centuries
of privilege and skills. Awareness of
their own aristocracy is embedded so deep
that only the genes need remember.
After all, there's no-one else
who's anyone. Here,
"county" counts for nothing, "town" is beyond the pale.

Unlike the roundups for Treblinka, Birkenau,
there are no uniforms in sight,
no enemy on that side of the gaze.
Twentieth century technology
has lost the skill to hide the agents,
but then canvas was scarce in the ghettos
and needed for body bags. Holocaust photos
show human faces. The camera lies
heavy on our conscience, heavier than paint.

Gentlemen hunt foxes. Possums, no matter
how renardine they're made to look,
being edible, are lesser game.
Naked and sexless as apes, their skin
fur-brown, the Palawa
are unwitting intruders in this Henry Alken scene,
their homes folded comfortably over fallen logs,
their fires not yet at crematorium heat.

Low Tide

The land's subservient to the sky, the sea even more so
yet it controls, provides the mirroring heart
in pools left as mementos of power.
Despite the rocks' romantic finger
pointing, as usual, towards the ineffable,
the good old ineffable, standby of scapes that would sweep
you past the frame and into light,
that white band snaps you back.

The sky's hegemony is only spatial.
Where the coarser, calmer brushstrokes groove and
stripe the light in angles no nimbus should have
it says, "You wouldn't want to know about the weather."
Lower, a more acceptable truth
asserts itself in a flurry of cumulus and light touches.

Light touches the windless pools, too,
spins back from their flatness
skipping diminuendo through the clouds.

Why would a man come here to play
aesthetic ducks and drakes, bound and re-
bound paint until you'd think the unseen sun
had made this out of vibrations and nothing else?

The urge to con, the need to be seen as source,
cool god-games, the old ineffable again.

The gulls are not gulled by this, forage
around weed the green of ancient copper,
dive against reflected light.

Fruit and Flowers

Still life? At first only the frame sings with the zing
of fruit, pours its juice of light into one corner,
to sustain objects detached from sap,
cut and culled away from life to art.

The optimistic English translates to French
as *nature morte*, dead fruit still edible,
dead blooms still fresh with garden colour.
At what stage do picked things die, become
art, decoration, food? If there's no heart, no brain
to stop, what's the point
at which only the artist can save an inert bunch
from being dead boring?

Why, for that matter, do we say "dead boring"
as if death did not fascinate us
at least as much as art and life
and almost as much as where they interface?

A ranunculus is a ranunculus is . . .
as Stein could have said (but didn't,
roses being more accessible and more
euphonic), and people who like paintings of flowers,
Cocteau said, love flowers and hate art.

But the painted image of a stem
is not a stem, as those old modernists
should have known ("*Ceci n'est pas une pipe.*")

The aim was not to elicit saliva or tears,
for the peaches trying not to look
too human and indelicate, almost succeeding,
nor for Sweet Williams like targets but not quite dead centre.
(That's called "interesting composition" and shows
the artist was "imaginative".)

Still less for strawberries, one up, one down,
like the masks that advertise amateur dramatics
in 1850 drawing rooms, or like
the terrace houses of the working class.
Half ripe, if bitten they would only yield
the sweeter, livelier part, nearer the base,
once the tough tip had been spat out.

Nor were we meant to drool
for gooseberries veined like a pair of eyes,
grapes black and white with hyacinths to match,
an idealist's symmetry of seasons.

These are rather foods and flowers for thought,
for meditating on the best of both worlds,
both dimensions of the framed plane, dark and bright,
swinging on the century's hinge, still and alive.

Sunday in the Gardens

Little Miss Licorice Legs, fling the sky today,
lob the sunlight up behind the hedge
and let it bounce where the smallest dancing kids
are no more than extra dapples,
a blossom froth of muslin.

Today the future doesn't bulk
like nursemaids dull as duty. Not yet
will a gent, the cut of his coat a dance itself,
try to win your smile from beneath a flowered hat.
Today it's a gift to the air.

The garden steps are stripes of sun.
They lead up from innocence.

Naming the Sensation No 2

> *"Girls just want to have fun."*
> — Cyndi Lauper

Rothko died from an overdose
of mystic seriousness and Clyfford Still
rode, lone, the rim of his own spirit's ranch.

JP, of course, romanticised
biochemistry and his muscles,
mistaking both for power, got it wrong.

Barney Newman won the Cold War,
his stripes like a sergeant's or a flag's,
art's own John Wayne in Sensurround.

Motherwell can't place quite all
the blame on Freud, who taught him that
boys just want to have angst.

Paint as bourbon, semen, sweat,
the quest, the thrust: the galleries
confused testosterone with art.

Half of humanity meanwhile
was object, suffixed by De Kooning's
Roman numerals, or hid outside

the rich white cube of fame, head down,
bum up and waiting, either for or on.
Now at last we all can see

the world through rosy TV screens,
more *Rage* than rage, a festival
of clips and chats, layers of cathode pink

as taffeta, lip gloss giving lip,
a nub of candy in the purse, the pulse
engulfing, innermost delight.

Humpty Dumpty and Taxidermy

for John Wolseley

Who else would be brave enough to try
putting Gondwana together again
when all the king's horses etc. lacked the art?
There's more than one way to unscramble this omelette earth.

Now all our eggs are in the one hemisphere
we are meticulous with shell,
solving tectonic puzzles grass by grass,
one femur at a time.

Before the fall
even the fauna was colonised.
Wombats were stuffed to look like toothless beavers,
sitting up in comic poses.

Heads of African antelopes today
are stored discreetly out of the line of fire
but still collared by their wall-mounts
waiting for ressurection with the den.

Where is the collection of firearms kept?
There should be rows of racks, a squadful.
to remind us that our heritage is the explosion
of continents.

Sydney Cove

Coppered up to the bends so pirates would think her
HMS, but with iron fastenings,
she was sailing for electrolytic disaster
even before the Forties roared between her timbers.

When trade poses as government
the effects reach even the remotest of
"the humbler class of islands" in an unknown strait
and stay there, outlasting scurvy and storms.

The prices paid for what was saved
and sold in Sydney were "most enormous":
twenty-two shillings for a cup and saucer.
How much is that in bodies below the anchor deck?

What never needed salvaging
was drowned capital's concretion
thick around holes the shape of lives
corroded away for the profits of an agency house.

Campbell and Clark bought naming rights
to history, which does not record
the lascars except as a job lot.
We have the rum, the shoes, the indigo

rescued, restored, identified.
We have that other commodity, life,
still bought cheap as ballast
in the name of enterprise.

Bound to Please

Tiny cranes twined with butterflies,
silk on silk on skin on broken bone:
a life embroidered into symbol,
the whims of lust calcified to code,
can stand on its own two emblems of class and sex,
but only just, its contact with the earth
no more than palace dancers have,
cranes of good fortune or butterflies.

All the whales have gone from the Bay of Biscay
for stays to shape the fantasies of men
under Coutille or broché by Nuform,
the Elastiline Reduso, the Nautilus
or Liberty's latest range.
The S-bend and the hourglass have their uses
round any clean and punctual house
with firm foundations.

The stuttering gait of status,
the clamped lungs' shallow twists of breath
were not design faults. Allure
is always fashioned for control.

Led

We take our rituals with us even when we go
where they have never been.
Tea caddies lined with lead
protected the makings of Empire
as English parties advanced beyond
known lawns to fill their fine bone cups
with new infusions of familiar blends
strained through the whiskers of certainty.

Lead poisoning, we now know, destroys
the sense (among others) of direction.
How many intrepid surveyors,
heroic botanists, muscular missionaries,
stirred themselves anti- and clockwise
through the scrub till they dissolved?

Poems 1990–1999

Leipzig

Against Honecker's hoons
the *Gewandhaus* was sanctuary.
Masur stopped the show,
was a safe conductor.
Music, after all, formed
with Party and Sport
the Trinity.

Now *Deutschland über Alles*
in the square drowns out Bach
and Irving's apologia for Adolf
proves freedom of speech.
Where is the sanctuary
for those who shot through
the wall to the dole queues?

A 14-year-old girl with
shoulders as big as all of Prussia
does lonely laps in water
clean of chemicals and blood
against the clock,
against the clock.

To Adrian Paunescu

This Summer of lies
from Murdoch and CBS
was your Winter of truth.

They trashed your villa,
pissed in your spa,
raped all your mistresses
with Coke bottles.
They will burn your books.

Another laureate
of the gilded left
was exiled there:
verse, luxury
velut crimen abhorred.

Metamorphoses:
subdued *vox populi*
to stag's troat;
"people's poet"
now, like Imelda's shoes
or Tammy's tears
a filler joke.

Empires today,
more scissile, less
able to withstand
the modish wowsers,
are easily replaced.
When the barbarians
come from the West
live via satellite
to what were satellites,
now centrifugally
at large, lassoable,
yet another (just what
the cowboy ordered)
Augustan age will spread
its bland and regular smog
over the provinces.

Raise your hand
and say after me:
"I want to buy.
I want the freedom
of brand names.
I want a Porsche
and a human right
and a ball-point pen
that really works.
Democracy's
the real thing."
Sign here.

Every age of course
should have its Alcaeus.
Eternal opposition
inspires, excites,
is good for an awkward laugh.
But it's a queer enough trade
that the toady, the hack
deserves a memorial.

The networks, the agencies
haven't kept us informed.
It's a queerer trade still
when our hypocrite doubles
write us cliff-hanging.
I'll take my pay, too,
now we are fellow citizens,
fellow exiles. Welcome,
one way or another, to
Nova Dacia. Pax.

Crash

The trackball judders.
The display rattles the screen.
Down past each lit window of the Exchange
what flutters cannot be read
aloud to the uninitiate.
No fireside oenomancy
saw this declension in the lees.

"Get out while you can"
is more in the nature of
kindly advice than imperative
while the addicts boot up
manic spreadsheets on their laptops
and laugh as the marina
acquires gaps like a row of Bosnian terraces.

In the tabloids life goes on
nobly. Under the gilt aluminium
coaching lamps the wine list is heavy.
Smart is the aim, the theory,
but after hours it comes down to
the usual, thanks. We promise ourselves
that tomorrow we shall read the signs.

The Living are Left with Imagined Lives

i.m. Robert Harris

You will not add age's load to wisdom's.
It would have been superfluous, anyway,
best left for those who need a longer lease.
You carried, you said, the sins of the city
on your shoulders, no bed or desk so awkward
that the lies it had produced could not be straightened
round the narrowest stair-turnings of the heart.

So much that hasn't died sings darkly:
Piaf's hollow bones as flutes for fire,
each albatross rigging the clouds with wit,
the sweat and comity of useful work,
scraps of sad Jane wherever light meets stone,
but, mostly, love tough as the skin on old words
yet still too slippery for the nets
the honest eclipse has dropped between us.

"A million golden birds of future vigor"
you wished me once. What skies of mine they've graced
have been the more open for the memory
of your discourse, its hard innocence,
of courage lacking calculation,
your blunt face butting at the truth.

Cold War

The forties, that avuncular decade:
Not only Joe and Walt, one at each shoulder,
but all those other uncles back from the war that took fathers,
lounging by motor-cars in wide-trousered suits,
the childless ones that always swung you highest,
the slightly fabulous, the mildly crude,
the one who could fart the "Reveille"
and the slim, worried one with a face
firm and smooth as a cigarette from an art deco pack.

There were aunts, of course, and cousins
who were never quite as real as neighbour kids.

But it was the uncles who were in tune
with the years of Hoagie and Bogie,
of boogie and childish hunting, hiding games.

When the Saints Go Marching Out

> "When the unbeliever asks about your faith, take him
> to the church and show him your icons"
> — Eighth Century Russian saying

> "Give me back the Berlin Wall.
> Give me Stalin and Saint Paul.
> I've seen the future, baby. It is murder."
> — Leonard Cohen

Sofya Andreyevna, born when the red day broke,
now 75, arthritic, lies on the floor
of the Church of the Annunciation, Zaluch'ye.
Basil, George, the Archangel Michael,
her name-saint Sophia and even
the Virgin in gold are gone from the wall.

"Painted by Rublev himself" the village knew.
"After the style of . . ." art historians
almost concurred. In due time
at Christie's or Sotheby's someone will decide.
The market will give them a real value.
For half a millennium they warded off
the wolves of doubt and reason.

*Multiple fractures to the skull
caused by repeated blows with a heavy object.*

Blood and hair on the silver candlestick
found in the snow by the fresh tyre tracks.

Sofya Andreyevna will survive
and in the few years left, remembering
siege, lack, terror, ice, will know
that none of them was strong enough to rip
her faith away like this.

Love Poem for Stephanie

When we talk it should be
in Cocoliche or Baracoon,
some creole we can live in,
built from the tentative pidgin
of cultures touching lightly
like trade, like skin, learning
each other, working past
getting and giving to love.

When we move there should be
strange names for what we do
towards each other. No dance,
gambit or skater's leap
is new enough to make
such unnatural demands
on the lexicon of contact
and release, trust and surprise.

Don Gibson and Etymology

The other night, listening to "Sea of Heartbreak",
I picked up on the word "caress".
It is, of course, cognate with
"charity" and "whore" and the Latvian
kars, meaning "randy".

                        "Memories of . . ."
fingernails light on the lower back,
the Smith Family building set among
Joe Borg's brothels—East Sydney '68.

". . . so divine." Well, a good ol'
C & W boy can be excused
for confusing the divine
with the desirable.

                        The song
goes on: "How I wish . . . "
I'm on dry land, on a mountain,
in a room full of dictionaries.
Cars are for driving, for ferrying across water,
and no-one speaks Latvian any more.

Erechtheus 33's Apologia

for Mark Davis

I posted my modernism by snail-mail, dropped it in
the humanist slot in the box that didn't have
E II R on it any more. Gough mit uns.
It was addressed "Dear Reader", an anagram for
er, er, er, Dada. Iconoclasm
is being smashed again. I never got around
to buying a TV. Gilligan's Island
was more remote than Santa Catalano,
"26 miles across the sea". A bunch
of Bradys that didn't include Matt
or Veronica might as well have been
the Mangoplah-Cookardinia United
half-back line or the offspring of
the drover's wife and the drover's dog.

Now they say Ern Malley and Detective Vogelesang
were on the same team. Cultural theory,
conspiracy theory: someone's not
the full denko and it might well be me.
The absence of Martin Bryant jokes tells us
that the line is always drawn somewhere,
but by whom? Gatekeepers, drunken porters—
Hal, Peter, Dorothy or Prêt à—
"Eat up your whalemeat and don't blubber
about the El Niño effect, the Sal Mineo effect
or how green is Green Valley," they still warn me.
When I was an Argonaut I never got
a Blue Certificate and I never quite made it
as a bodgie. Can I join your gang?

Poem for Port Arthur

... where the cricket ground still shines like a brass thingummy
on an eager ensign's jacket
and muslin waves lap irony at the stone.
Diana never came here, but it doesn't matter.
By '96 romantic stories had long given way
to Convict Barbie and the Pentax Penitentiary.
This is a history of the urge to make a quid
and its consequences. Alf Maule would tap
with his walking stick *the very spot* on the flags
which a deed apocryphal even to Marcus Clarke
had stained. Alf and the other guides had the patter
as glib as a politician's response to massacre.

One of them, Jim MacArthur, had burned down the church
then made a living describing its remains.

Interpretation has always been the problem.
No wonder, when the press needed to doctor
electronically the killer's eyes. As if
the memory of picnic outings by steamer
for charitable causes wasn't enough.

Sunlight on the green or the weather off Cape Raoul
huge as empire: we still deny it all,
waiting for the next *son et lumière*, which will descend
like a princess.

Aerodynamics

The field where Wittgenstein flew his kites
behind The Grouse, high above sheep
and Glossop, is now a helipad.
He would have understood the use
of the tourism text, even though the rotors
in chopping the traces of clear currents
are not there, as I am, in homage
to clear thought. Views of the Peak District,
thirty quid a spin, stranded hikers
lifted from ontology and snow.

Ah, the kites, the winds of Kant, the answer
blowing on the moors!

Theory trudges in to The Grouse's snug
and orders a pint of Thwaites.
Doctrine and method foam together
while the sleet drives in from Heptonstall
across the bitter valley, across
the kiteless black air from Sylvia's grave
where language functions on a simple card,
anonymous: "With love" in a small hand.
Beyond logical necessity, the absence of kites
flies like a tautology screaming in the gale.

Below the weather commerce scrawls
propositions between mills and learning.
Love and stone wear each other. Words
bear all our kites and shape our air.

Speaking for Myself

i.m. Brett Whiteley

You gave me the American Dream
I had already been dreaming,
portraits of shared heroes,
dared lines, sweet games.

You drowned me through the ultramarine
of my harbour, exploded me
—palm tree or lion—terrible
as brain, river, sex, flight, self.

You took my addictions,
curved them into your blood,
swirled mushroom waves, the beaks
and hills, the alchemy of need.

Now I have to see round corners
for myself. What I see
is the full warm promise
of an empty motel room,

the air and debris fidgeting
with infinity, the trick perfumed
and sacred, waiting. I hang between
redemption's con and courage.

The Aisles

> *"In Greece, he'd sing some sort of hymn like this t' ye:"*
> Byron, Don Juan, Canto III

The poets and postcards were right.
The Aegean is as blue as Toilet Duck,
but I wouldn't drink wine that shade of dark.

On Hydra, "le Johnston de nos jours,"
I soak up my own light aura of pretension
along with the retsina splashed by sun

and play at being the poet playing at
being the tourist. This is by way of
a snapshot greeting from the isles

where burning Byron . . . and you know the rest,
including the history of the one island
which consistently sold out,

to the Venetians, the Turks and now the Yanks.
And Karamanlis died today,
le Menzies de leurs jours.

So I drink at the Sun Set Bar
halfway between Disco Heaven
and the yacht club's bikinis

and watch the wakes, like chips of temple marble,
slice neat as Visa cards across the path
of Phoebus plunging with his dazzling trolley.

"Yet in these times he might have done much worse:"
George's irony was less cliff than balcony.
The view's still clear, the octopus delicious.

Liberation's not a phallic ruin,
a flag-stripe against the sky,
a flush of azure on the porcelain.

The world's shelves are wiped
clean as sunlight. They are stocked
with meditations on antiquity.

Brontë Country

I swear I saw Branwell, young again,
in a pub in Haworth through the karaoke crowd.
I remembered Doris Leadbetter's story of the village drunk
who sat in the corner "an' Branwell were the village drunk before me
an' this were 'is chair." This dark-curled American tourist, all Pre-
    Raphaelite
and solitary with his bitter, not playing the pokies and definitely not
looking at the historical prints of railway scenes as monochrome as the
    skyline,
TV antennae and all, on a day no brighter than the parsonage,
sat, still as the couch on which Emily died but better preserved,
his eyes the colour of the tumbling gravestones up on the hill
or the shadows that hide, waiting for the sunlight
when they will skid like fictitious siblings,
a source of visible delight
but unneccesary.

Mother and Son

It's March again, our month. Now
it's a different hospital, a different city.
We talk above the nebuliser's roar:
part chainsaw, part surf, all edge.

The spasms of pain are at closer intervals
as you labor, this time to postpone
the separation. Your skin's cross-stitched
with butterflies and bruises.

Your hands, which I never heard play Poulenc,
never fast enough, you said,
grip, but mine keep slipping
as I slipped away from you those years ago.

Holding on isn't always everything. Skin slides.
Too tough to die, too proud to call this living,
you hug into these punctuated hours
our missed half-century of love.

For My Father

My friends are writing elegies for their fathers.
I have so much to say about you, and memories
have nothing to do with it. We never met.
You have conned me even more effectively
than all your other gulls and marks.
You conned me into being. Forty years
I held you dead hero or at least Kilroy.

Then when you really died I became
your ghost. Your hairline, chin and gait
returned to haunt those who barely mourned,
while you still con me and I fall for it
again, giving you life.

                      No doubt you wore
the Flying Officer's uniform more dashingly
the night you conned my mother than I wear
your face and limbs. Nothing I have written
has had a punchline half as sharp
as Grandmother's signature when you put it
on your prize fiction work, her will.

Did you ever imagine my fantasies,
and was that why you had all those medals
no-one ever won who never left
Sale or Laverton except on leave or awol?
We picked the same *Boys' Own* stories
to not grow out of.

         Once I wrote,
"Seeking heroics, we become absurd."
But that was about me. You found heroics
easy as any pose: judge, doctor, engineer.
Post-modern before your time, you had
more style than Walter Mitty. Once you shaped up
against an angry neighbour who had inches,
stone and skill on you. He backed away.

I've swapped audacity for irony.
You never pretended to be
anything less than excellent.
No wonder you could not acknowledge me.

Keeping the Dream Alive

The place is full of jealous whingers
who want to cut down the tallest poppy
in the trade. Together we can pull through this,
mate. Maaaateship. I love to have a beer with Lawsy, 'cos . . .
There's too many of you out there
not pulling your weight, not game enough
to get behind the banks.
You've gotta be game, game as . . .
Does Westpac still have a branch at Jerilderie?
Talk back to an ATM with a seven second delay,
which is longer than it took for Ned to say
"Such is life" or Red Barry to gong him
off *Hey Hey It's the Nineteenth Century*.

And I say this, Australia:
If we don't all, in the best Aussie tradition,
get in there and pass the hat round for the shareholders
of our great financial institutions,
there's no hope for us as a decent nation
and the shooting of Sergeant Kennedy at Stringybark Creek
might just as well have been any other Kennedy death.
Sid Nolan's paintings will be lined up against the wall and
hung
then sold for $1.2 million
and whose vault will it be that they go into?
Ah, Snowtown, heart of Australia, where they keep
the welfare bludgers off the streets
with a little help from the ANZ
and a little help from the NAB
and the Commonwealth,
because wealth is so common
that you and I, Australia, can afford to watch it,
our greatest spectator sport since public executions.

from *aUStralia* (2004)

Oosutoraria

> "... in the whole world there is not a worse country"
> —Major Robert Ross, 1788

> "... the kokakoala bear/for mascot..."
> —Selwyn Pritchard, 2000

So nature's arse-about. It has to be
where birds are blood-bright for camouflage
among the deeds and trophies the National Trust
and National Party hallow. The black swan
of impasse has its season now and then,
is vice-regally shot, Game's game, anyone's cur
for the price of a drink. Our heritage:
the sailors of the *Sydney* who sang like kangaroos,
Pearce's Lewis gun detachment, defeated
by a platoon of emus in '32, out West.
Now that the Lion has lain down with the Lam-
borghini the fauna can stand proud
with cultural identity, Mickey and Minnie
by the plagueful, Easter Bunnies enough
to turn the paddocks the colour of milk chocolate,
and natives, too, the scissor-wielding dingo
of Uluru, a six-pack of fairy penguins
(easier to carry), on Rottnest a game
of quokka soccer. When the thylacine
smiles now we know it's not only because
the brewery got its tail wrong on the labels.

Progress is not passé, even in Adelaide.
By the end of the millennium no headland
will be without a concrete toilet block.
New tar shouts on the road like Texan wealth
all the way to Jewel. On the box
smiles are tight lycra and, look again,

those aren't tears but sweat drops
as the steroid republic pumps its way
to the starting block. If you're sent off
for snarling "bloody Mabo" to the ref
you can always appeal. Just remember
to hold the akubra more or less over
your heart when they play anything by Peter Allen
as you blink at the top of the flagpole.

No smartarse mentions angst down at the Rissole.
Angst is a silent cliff, its vastness
easily swallowed by a shouldered Sony or the yawn
of a motel desk-clerk reading Laissez Murray
in the original English.

We remember every 25th of April
that Australia doesn't rhyme with success
and there's an autographed Fairlie Arrow poster
even in the Last Resort.

Vinegar Hill

Across the Blue Mountains lay the fabled lands,
Tir na-n'Og and Hy Brasil, Mac Con Glinne's realm
where everything is made of food. The eternal West
of Celtic heaven called to the croppy boys in hell.

"Pikes, pikes! We'll plant the Liberty Pole
in King's garden, finish in New South Wales
what we started in Wexford, live forever!"
But General Holt preferred to lick English spittle.

So with Cunningham at Castle Hill
less than a thousand of "the most wild,
ignorant and savage Race" faced death
not liberty, but not before some fun.

They dragged the flogger, Duggan, out
from where he curled, squeaking, under his bed,
a mouse for the cat. "United Irishmen"
was a poor joke. The newly united kingdom

had more solidarity, had onside
the tired and the toadies, had the last laugh
when the lads ran up against Laycock,
who in his bright boots was six foot six

"and he could not get any higher as he took
blood money in England." Even the petty sycophant,
Ruse, "natef of Cornwell", stood too high,
while that long squirt of piety,

Marsden, over the triangle, under the flag,
his bible squat and dark as a rum bottle,
cast a shadow longer than a gun
on grass too wretched ever to be green.

Pinchgut

Mattewanye had been a rock
of oysters and fun, sacred
to salt slitherings on picnics.
When the men in strange skins came,
their faces the colour of galahs,
they put a corpse up there, the dead flag
of a man called Morgan, who'd used
his cooper's hammer to tap into
half a pint of rum through someone's skull.

Flapping in chains it was meant as
a warning, was more an ensign.
Mattewanye has been boarded
by death and now sails on the harbour
under a sun that dries gunpowder
on water that tastes of gunpowder,
crewed by the doubly exiled
who starve there, guts pinched by salt.
Generations who'd slurped pleasure there
will never go back. It's fit for
a storehouse, a fort or a clock.

Spider Dance and Horse Whip

> "The symbol of innocence is the statue of Eve"
> — Lola Montez

The dance had little to do with innocence
or statues, but we get the point.
Eve is what she makes you make of her.
Lola spun the miners tight and sticky,
danced her nocent web lightly, shaking
its strands till they dazzled like the vein
through the Gravel Pits or the lines
that join the silver stars of the flag.

Each small muscle under the satin
skin or fleshy silk could, flexing, suck
a man's brains out through his cock
at ten yards distance. Every part of her
could pout an invitation.

Innocence is winning a horse whip
in a raffle and joking about critics.
A whip can dance eight-legged, light
over a bug-eyed face, can weave
red webs as rapidly as any editor
can boil and spit out "notoriety".

To whip up a stockade against the traps
of the flesh, against the trapdoor predator,
is useless. Innocence is a tricky art.
It can be spun on stage and stretched
to catch a full house or to tangle
one man's anger and a town's lust.

Mandarin of the Crystal Button

The *Afghan* lay in Sydney Harbour, hundreds
of Chinese passengers below decks,
a few tense guards. After the torchlight march
of 5,000 from the Town Hall, fired
by Ninny Melville, Norton and grog,
had forced a note from Parkes that he would break
the law and keep them out—the birth
of the White Australia Policy that never was—
the press went on board and played their part
by telling the cops that the Chinese would eat them.

Quong Tart ate no-one but, like any other
British gentleman, he ate this land,
gorged on his Araluen Eldorado,
having arrived aged nine and skinny
on the fields, grew with the tea trade,
joined the Masons and the Oddfellows,
umpired at cricket, wore kilt and sporran.
"I never thought Lord Carrington
was so dark complexioned," someone said
on seeing him with other dignitaries.

Quong Tart went on board the *Afghan*,
worked a deal over a cuppa,
kept everyone sweet (enough to eat),
said later, "I like Britis' race alright, my word!"
died when one of them mugged him for twenty quid.

The Policy continued to non-exist
for 80 years of white tea with sugar.

Coningham v Coningham

As the colonies were uniting,
Arthur was divorcing Alice.
The co-respondent had been recommended
to Cardinal Moran by the Pope himself:
Father O'Haran. Fiercely prot,
Arthur only wanted custody
of Alice's elder two, plus cash
for damages. The third he said was fathered
when she was Fathered. The revolver
he fired in the court when he lost the case
had been loaned to him by William Dill Macky,
the Presbyterian Gunman.

But Moran missed out on precedence
over the C of E on New Century's,
New Nation's Day thanks to the scandal.
The gunman, too, was miffed that his lot
weren't up there with Archbishop Smith and co.
So there weren't any Micks or Jocks at the do
and for weeks the sermons were thunderbolts
splitting the cobbled country into more than states.

Black Cat and Wooden Shoe

Joe Hill "wouldn't be found dead in the state of Utah"
so his ashes went to Wobblies round the world.
Australia's portion was siezed in a raid
before it could be decently interred
in the Botanical Gardens, ended up
in the fireplace of Central Police Station, Sydney,
not keeping the coppers nearly hot enough
so they warmed up by running through the streets
scraping off walls Tom Barker's poster,
the one urging bosses, parsons, editors
and landlords to war and workers to follow them.

It got hotter still when Tom was jailed.
Simpson's Bond Store, Stedman's, Winn's
all burned as beacons of war-bond investment,
Bryant and May the opposition spokesmen
for liberty. Better fire than blood,
or let the politicians cut their own throats
to dowse the flaming struggle.

Lockout

Next-door were lucky; they had cookery books,
read recipes around the table when they were hungry.
We didn't even have that. It was scab or starve.
John Brown had said, "Let them eat grass."
We held out. Dad was solid. Mum was a bunch of twigs.

Most of them were returned men, too, the ones
that were fired on at Rothbury, but some were kids,
or older, too slow or too naive to be safe,
like the old bloke who looked like he was tied
to the roadside gravel by a skein of blood

from his stomach, trying to push himself up,
or the young feller with two bullets lodged
in the loose skin under his jaw. But he survived,
which is more than our Norm did
after the dum-dum got him in the guts.

Cessnock lost 25 cricket teams thanks to
the lockout. Men who'd come through
Gallipoli, Salonika, the Dublin Post Office
or jail as COs only to be shot by Aussies found
if they won't let you work, you can't afford to play.

You know a town is really desperate
when the evangelists come to scavenge.
They filled one of the pits with water,
turned it into a great baptismal bath
to save whole families for John Brown's Jesus.

The Mayor

after Frank Hardy

When his missus had shot through
just before the Duke of Gloucester's visit
he needed a Lady Mayoress for the reception,
so hired a prostitute. She passed OK except
when she hitched up her skirt
and had a snake's in the hand basin.
After all, the Duke wouldn't have known
one working class colonial from another
and the Duchess kept her gloves on,
didn't need to wash her hands.

Then there was the time he drove
the Council's steamroller into the Yarrra,
got a three hundred quid commission
on the sale of a new one. Fair enough
for a chuckle over a few gins years later.
He even steamrolled Wren's machine
and Keon's and the Left to make
a building site for independence
in the inner suburbs. Local government
today is corporate, slick as soapy water,
plays Pilate to the old rorts.

But what the municipal incinerator burned
besides the waste from backyard abortions
and pre-selection ballot boxes
from unreliable wards, we'll never know.
"*Non corpus delicti*" Squizzy used to say—
"No corpse, no bloody inquest".
What do we wash our hands in when
we avoid judgement or before
we clap them or slap our thighs
for the larrikin battler and his heirs?
Are we sure it's sweeter than a whore's piss?

Tanah Merah

A pencilled note thrown
to the wharf at Bowen from the *Both* was
a gap of white in the green curtain,
a peep-hole in hell's back door,
a scribbled PS to 20 years
of a future nation's leaders isolated
in "a specially appointed place"
malarial, rotting, ringed by ravines,
escape-proof. Thousands had been sent,
intellectuals, unionists, whole families.
Hundreds survived.

Was it chance their first landfall was Paterson's town?
Even miles up the Digul a wharfie knows where his mates are,
knows that despite the pink skin, big noses, foreign smell,
the angle of the bent backs is the same,
that not all blonds are bastards.
They would soon find out that in this country
not all bastards are bastards,
but those that are are real bastards.

When Mynheer Dr Van Der Plas
came up the Digul to address
his "fellow-countrymen"
and ship them to Australia,
he said he liked the Indonesian people.
So did the cannibals in the jungle around the camp.
The old and the sick were left.
Their deaths would not help the Japanese.
Australia had always been a safe place
to put superfluous humanity. It had been
a century since the last load.

Advent: 21 Dec. 1967

In St Pauls the play
re-enacted and rehearsed a birth
while through and around the faithful audience
ASIO's backstage crew prepared
for the coming of LBJ
and his retinue of shepherds and crooks:
Thieu, Park, Marcos, Kittikachorn,
whose lambs had been stuck and left to spurt
all over South-East Asia
till the undertow of blood was stronger than Cheviot,
sucked and ripped more life more fiercely.

The wise men, by the way, stayed away,
responding to the appeal
by Police Commissioner Arnold:
"No demos by request".

This was the fifth day. The surf
had trundled nothing up, rolled no rocks aside.
Sea lice can inside twenty-four hours
stuff themselves with every morsel
of what makes the difference
between a PM and a skeleton.
By now they would be working on
the ligaments. By Tet there will be
unconnected bones.

You can't shoot sea lice with a speargun,
or bomb the tide away.

Sight Screen

When Kim Hughes's tears
hardened to cataracts
only the gleam of rands
provided enough light to take guard
as the umpire gave him two legs.
He never got his eye in again.

Two legs are not enough to avoid
being run out by dogs and mace.
Blindness is only a virtue in justice,
or else black and white look unalike
and a keen eye can pick out
a lethal delivery against a coloured crowd.

And now the laager louts are in,
cutting and glancing to the darkest boundaries
of sponsors' visions, piling on the runs:
another Great Southern Stand to cheer.
What is the sawdust soaking up
on the run-up to freedom?

The slow-mo replay keeps repeating
scenes where the red on clothes
doesn't come from polishing the ball.
No matter how advanced
the electronic scoreboard is
there are some sundries it can't record.

Poems 2000–2006

Et in Acadia Ego?

1. Bob Harris Real Estate, Cole Harbour NS

So should all the best poets be reincarnated.
Signs all over Eastern Nova Scotia
show that this time around
Bob is selling heaven in quarter-acre lots:
tiny islands with spruce grove and rowboat,
white clapboard house with red barn
and view of the Atlantic through mist
by a bream-glinting inlet
where two old men and a small girl
fish from the bridge for a whole tide
and don't mind not catching anything.
What's more, this time around
Bob's getting his fair cut.

2. Forbes, Dr John (GP) New Glasgow NS

Here's karmic reward for a healer of the mind,
and the pay's better: allergies, infections,
kids' tummyaches, certificates for sickies –
and there's plenty of those at the steelworks,
the paper mills, the Pioneer mine where the strike is two
      months long
and Bill Guthro was run into a ditch last Thursday
by a company front-end loader.
I know John'll fix him up as he fixed us all.
Dispensing jovial wisdom in a small town
must be a cinch after being a Sydney boy
trying to pick winners in compassionate Melbourne.

3. Salmon River Presbyterian Church. Minister: Rev. Andrew Hardy

Having refused, eloquently, to preach in Launceston
but having guided us over the city rooftops
and along the stencilled walls of wit
now the "defender of family values"
can strike a pose as snowy and neo-Gothic
as his wooden church and command
the respect denied tagless graffitists
and self-published poets no matter how
much genius is squeezed into the casual smile.
Thinking long and connected no longer,
let us pray. This, after all, is the next life.

Dry

"Bleached" grass (by some white king of science?)
or "blanched"? but anyway a fire hazard,
if hazard is not too tentative a word in February
for the pale invasive culture
we have introduced, will, if chance
roots among the shiny bulblets,
catch.

We hold as lightly as death
the living topsoil and hardly
the rock, but we are very good
with surfaces and glyphosate.

What is left to walk through,
however delicately placed each
of our RM Williams boots?
What you see. Every look kills.
Blind hazard, accidental sight
burn as much as they smother.

I think "blanching" (as if with fear, yet slightly active)
but I dare not be sure.

If I think like this summer hillside
what white distortions will I undergo?
Easier to ask, "What is to be done?"
(The passive either a cop-out
or hypocrisy) than to gamble
with answers in the onion twitch.

Zig-Zag Track

for CA Cranston

Go lightly on the dolerite.
Only a leap away from the lookout bedrock is
lower than sea level.
Where the high voltage wires
start across the gorge
the sign reads "instant death".
These days no-one takes the time to decay slowly
the way the rock forms soil.

The jointing pattern jumps from point to
point. From she-oak to native hop,
geniculate and furcular, difficult
as speech, simple as lines of air,
the cracks write no warning.
What Jurassic texts we might read
are translated by guess and mostly we start
from the scratch of nervous energy,
the need to mark, to sign:
"instant death", "be warned",
"here be . . ."

Electric and delicate, death
will click into place.

Scapeland

What did I see, 495.4 m above the estuary?
Not the encrusted life on the oyster shell,
not a single dotterel headfeather, nor even
the sheen of the shard of a curlew's egg.
I was too high to discern
individual strands of kelp or shopping bags.

The freeway stretched like a campaign ribbon
on the soft barathea breast of a uniform
beneath which the heart of a general
who loved his grandchildren and kept fit beat.
I saw the chilled cubes of apartment buildings
with names stolen from California and palm trees
hijacked from the comfort of deserts.

The water in sunlight gleamed
like a brand new digital camera making a frame,
finding the view, metering the light, creating art.

The land shaft, the Apex lookout like
a land ship: what price etymology?
How gilt is language's frame where
we choose what to overlook, what to blame?

Writing the World

Metaphor's glib: the poem as . . .
suicide bomber, detainee,
wild river. the problem always
to live the meaning, when to write
only is at best to catalogue
or preach, cop out at worst.

How to mean the land?
As stones and currawongs
write, as 80 grand a year
buys dissertations on texts
no laptop ever shone,
where does creating fit?

Beyond taxonomy, beyond
marketable terror,
honesty always lies
somewhere over the line.
Flying is facile. Walk,
roll, crawl beyond the pale.

Make a mark. Leave no sign
unturned. Carry your baggage out.
Avoid the easy paradox
and give no orders.
Respect what you re-use
and sing innocently.

In weather that would turn milk,
when waiting uses all strength,
take the estuary's voice
and the sour clouds' script;
be a consultant to the air,
amanuensis to the earth.

Meditation on Parliament House, Canberra, 2002

Among the free world's lesser bastions
it would be easy to miss this minor
bunker under the rammed earth, the sheepish
grass, where the descendants of Macarthur's
Spanish/South African mindless ovines
cringe still, waiting for the fleecing, the dip
and drench, the indignity of the dogs
yapping and yarding, the orders to jump,
if it were not for the sheet of flag, flat
against a sky too torpid even to
galvanise irony, a standard that
proclaims: "It is night in the motherland;
the stars are out against the deep blue;
they surround the flag that comforts, blankets.
Sleep and dream of super japes in Iraq."

And the sheep toss only lightly, aware
that the Bush is vastly empty, a void
of inanity more terrifying
even than their own inbred Merino
aristocratic blankness, pure and white.

Elegance

I started an egret from the swampy flats
but not until I'd got as close
as I could, anyway, in street shoes
(lace-up, low-cut, German, matte black).
The bird stretched, elastic, beak up,
feet still as if caught under wet grass,
then it snapped into flight across the Nepean.

This was not my country. Trees I couldn't name
had dropped branches across the track.
Strange flowers were offered by the weeds.
Boral had put up a sign banning entry,
promising all kinds of accidents.
I thought of the comfort, the certainty
afforded by an Armani suit.

In Rome or Melbourne, sipping a single malt
with tall friends, I can read the landscape.
Here, there is no-one to answer my questions
even by e-mail though I have cried out
from my laptop, smooth and white as an egret.

Chemically Sharpened

for Bob Adamson

You split the squid for bait until
the esky lid was splotched with more dead ink
than yesterday's *Australian*.
The hooks are chemically sharpened. We wondered how.
You slid the snell until the dead squid would hang
life-like; jewies are hard to con, you said.
Just because they're big doesn't mean they're not smart.
Satisfied the elegant hooks were lined up
in pairs as convincingly as a headline
and its photo when the story's not biting,
you threaded the squid straight as a paragraph.

The moon came up strong over Lion Island.
We swung emptily around as the tide turned.
The jewies were not there — or not fooled.
We hauled in the cut corpses of squid
and sped back, the Haines Hunter tipping the wake's arrow
as if it had been chemically sharpened.
The newspaper had another report from Iraq.

Mesopotamian Suite

1. ACE

In September 2002 the White House Chief of Staff,
Andrew H Card Jr, when asked by reporters
why the US had not yet invaded Iraq,
answered, "From a marketing point of view,
you don't introduce new products in August."

Andy, when the chips, as they say, are down,
I want you in my hand or up my sleeve.
Not even your boss, the joker, for all his bluff
could deal a line as wild as that:
the spin on the spin on the spin.

While we wasted millions of non-combatant words
on pedantic points of morality or strategy,
while we marched or debated, worried or cheered,
you showed a sensitivity in tune with the turning year
like a nature poet or General Motors executive.

Some of us never learn. My last book was launched
in August. It didn't sell anywhere near as well
as Shock and Awe nor did it sever as many limbs.
Perhaps if I piled the critics in a naked pyramid . . .
But then that August thing is for the Northern Hemisphere,
    right?

2. FALLUJAH FACE-OFF, APRIL 2004

Scared teenagers steal hubcaps
off the war machine and know
only religion and danger.
There hasn't been time to learn

the history of last year's war,
let alone of this year's peace.
They cannot trust their officers
but they can be sure of Allah and of pain.

Across the two-lane blacktop
Justin Timberlake and Britney Spears
stand wide-eyed in battle fatigues
on a flat desert page from an atlas
they never opened. The flag and the music
provide the substance of their faith.
Their weapons are heavy but they get
regular e-mails from their pastors.

Alongside the road runs a pipeline
full of thick, black democracy
at $40 a barrel. It is oblivious,
having been dead for millions of years.

3. Two Purty Gals from West Virginia

Jessica, we all pentagonised
over your fate; we heard about
the stab wounds and the rape,
the evil doctors and the rescue
with cameras blazing. And now
we sympathise with your amnesia.
Children adorn your Internet shrines
with bad poems. There is no doubt
that you are the most photogenic Pfc
ever to be lied about for a bad cause.

Lynndie, we can forgive
the pointing finger, the leash, the cheeky grin,
but not the spelling of your name.
You were only following orders.
They weren't even Americans.
But what were your parents thinking?

4. Shake 'n' Bake

"*Gingerbread White House: View of the North Portico, 100 pounds (34 sheets) of gingerbread, 150 pounds of white and dark chocolate, Clear, poured sugar windows, One strand of white lights inside the Gingerbread White House make it glow.*" —White House Press Release, Christmas 2005

Make it glow. Make it glow. Make it glow.
White phosphorus over Fallujah, a hundred times sheet lightning:
the *illuminati* stagger out,
ripping away clothes, skin.
What were handfuls of flesh pour between fingers.
Breathing fluid fire, the too-bright smell,
they are not dead. Thirty seconds, forty-five,
then the high explosive follow-up
and all their Christmases come at once,
as the saying goes.

Every child knows about the witch in the gingerbread house,
about the glow from ovens.
Jenna and Barb jr are too grown-up
to play "knock-knock" at the sugar panes, to dare each other.
Fairy tales belong to the land
of faraway, of Scheherazade, saved by stories,

whose statue in Iraq has not been toppled.
Her saying goes and goes. She goes, "Onceuponatime..."
There was a city. A strand of white lights
made it glow.

5. The Code of Hammurabi

The Code of Hammurabi, once king of these parts, says:
"If anyone bring an accusation of any crime before the elders,
and does not prove what he has charged,
he shall, if it be a capital offence charged,
be put to death." When in Mesopotamia
do as the Mesopotamians do.
GWB. WMD. QED.

6. Baghdad Bazaar

What's on special today? Human life is still going cheap.
You can get Democracy in a special cut-rate package.
The voting bit has been taken out because the customers
would never get the hang of how to use it.

Sovereignty's a giveaway. Part of the label's come off
but if you look hard you can read the bit that says,
"... as long as you do what you're told."
What's that? No, we don't stock Reconciliation.

You could buy a used flying carpet from Chalabi.
The clock's only been wound back to 1978
and it's very light on gas, which is just as well
as we don't actually own any these days.

What do you mean you'll shop around?
We already have your credit card details
in the computer. You can expect a visit.
Now, how about some cheap antiquities?

7. Alabama

> "I got my kills, I'm coming down. I just love my job."
> — Sergeant James Anyett,
> US 1st Infantry, Fallujah, 2004

Last year it was whitetail in Barbour County,
the smell of pines and blood sweet as youth.
Daddy got my first kill mounted
as a 21st birthday present.
When my three littl'uns grow up
I'll take them to where the breeze off Lake Eufaula
makes you glad to be an Alabamian
and teach them manhood, teach them
about the subtle differences between
Remingtons and Winchesters.

There are no longleaf pines here, no yellowhammers,
but I've got my buddies; I've got better gear
than back home even and I'm being paid.
Bagged five this morning. Goddam shame
they won't let you take them home as trophies.
Although a couple were undersize and one was pregnant,
but those're just as hard to hit as the big buck towelheads.
They were going to bring in mortars, but I said:
Dude, give me the sniper rifle. I can take them out.
I'm from Alabama.

8. Purrfect Angelz

> *"Our performers are highly trained with years of*
> *experience and a positive attitude."*
> — Purrfect Angelz website

They went down well at the Full Throttle Biker Rally.
Now they're in Baghdad for the boys.
They sing. They dance. They acrobatise.
They wear . . . well, not much really,
but the hotpants are in regulation army colours.

Dayna, Deena, Monet and Shay Lyn
are spreading for the delectation of the troops
the values of the homeland, arousing
morale, reminding us of all the metaphors
of war and lust, and of a woman's place.
Re-energised after the show,
our highly trained personnel
go back to Abu Ghraib and put
their years of experience to work,
displaying a positive attitude.

9. And the Poets Fled

> *"And the poets fled, no longer able to think or sing*
> *in the midst of the horror."*
> — Tariq Ali

The cuneiform entries in Sumerian accounts
are still bleeding, wedges cut into the clay we are all made
   from,

notches keeping the score of harm and hope
from Ur to Halliburton's laptop screens
while history is written by arm-stumps in the sand
and rolls along the bottom of the CNN newscasts.

Where is the library of Sennacherib?
And who can read its books now?
And whatever happened to the Baghdad Poetry Festival?
The questions must assail the Green Zone like car bombs,
as insistent as the bare-handed crowds
who ripped collaborators apart in '58.

The poet Saadi Youssef wrote "The Jackals' Wedding"
from exile, sent it through cyberspace
faster than a Sidewinder and more deadly
to those who would never have sat at the jackals' wedding
    feast
whether it was the Medes or the Janissaries
or Negroponte who gave the bride away.

The poets will return. Saadi Youssef
will return as his poems already have.
Mudhaffar al-Nawab will return, and Sinan Antoon.
In the wine bars of Abu-Nuwwas Street we shall hear again
cluster-poems explode, watch heat-seeking poems
find their targets in the hearts and brains of friends.

South-Western Baptist

> "Behold, thou hast instructed many."
> —JOB 4:3

Paige Patterson sits among the heads
of pagan animals he couldn't convert.
For all the brash, Bush-ugly newness of the age,
one comfortable tradition remains;
the missionary/trader/hunter
still strolls the darker continents,
God's gardener, hand-in-hand with HIV,
culling for Christ and capital.

Teacher now, he jabs quotes, shoots
down Darwin; pro-choice gets Shock-and-Awe,
while freshmen suck on Scripture Mints™,
pledging big-eyed virginity:
no sweat-stains when they raise their arms
in lyre-shaped hosanna salutes.

Dr Patterson knows his appointed place:
between the angels and the elands,
lower than dead money, higher than
live flesh that rots in Sadr City gutters.

Meditations on Ms Westbury's Precepts

Poetry gives a sense of order and meaning.
My great-grandmother raised three sons:
one each for the army, medicine and the church.

Today's news: a young soldier hanged himself.
Great-Uncle Fred's order and meaning
were too much and not enough.

Grandfather's discipline saved lives, no doubt,
helped build the macho mystique of expertise.
This year's malpractice suits will all fail.

Great-Uncle Ernie's liturgies of love:
plainsong and incense fog the sound and sight
of decades of broken choirboys shuddering.

Order and meaning: I could add
teachers, a politician, journalists.
I hadn't realised the genes' resilience.

Metaphor has the power to stop us in our tracks . . .
Five US Marines were blown to chunks
when an insurgent reader refused to stop
for a metaphor on the road outside Mosul.

An overcrowded passenger train
between Seoul and Taejon yesterday
was derailed by a severe metaphor.
Two hundred casualties at latest count.

The only tracks I want to be stopped in
are the narrow-gauged lines that run
between order and meaning, laid down by poetry,
patrolled by poets in frightening uniforms.

Celebritocracy

You gotta have class. Only Marilyn Monroe,
Princess Di and a couple of Balkan war criminals
got their own "Candle in the Wind"
and even Marilyn had to wait.

The Saxe-Coburg-Gothas
and the Schleswig-Holstein-Sonderburg-Glücksburgs
and the Battenbergs of Hesse
used to have class. Now they have to marry it.

Should (Heaven forbid!) a barefoot yachting mishap
prove tragic, Our Mary would deserve more
than a new version of "Candle . . ."
Perhaps a revamp of "My Island Home".

Ever since the pretty princesses were spun
at us post-depression while we forgot
the jolly game of Dukes and Nazis
in a blur of tulle and fairytales,

the little girl in all of us
has clapped hands and danced
with sibling squabbles over whose turn it was
to be Lillibet or Margaret Rose.

Celebrity needs a context. Even Paris
wasn't built in a day. There has to be
a cast: the grumpy one in jodphurs,
the gin-soaked social climber with the dogs,

stock characters that prove
all the world's a sitcom:
the randy, the dotty, the stuttering reluctant,
even the locked-away gibberer.

Buckingham Palace and whatever it's called
in Denmark—Legoland—
are not quite Graceland or Ramsay Street
but as long as there's a princess there's hope.

Just keep the bulimia down and the details light.
Brunette is the new blonde. Plastic bags
are the new land mines. The candle, my friend,
is blowin' . . . but the times are unchanged.

Dentist's Waiting Room

Flicking through the mags checking the tsunami diet,
the asylum seeker's boob job and Terri Schiavo's horoscope,
I asked myself, "If Camilla can become Princess of Wales,
why can't Shane Warne be the next Pope?"
It would, of course, be more in keeping with tradition
if those roles were reversed, but let's not think too deeply
about such weighty matters; let's instead
amuse our winter selves with poolside skimming
through the glossy travel supplement of *Island*
imagining those cute poems with little umbrellas over them.
When *Ten Days of Ten Eighty* comes along I know it's time
to head for the intellectual stimulus of Port Douglas.
Pass the *history wars* brand sunblock and my
Reconciliation sarong, the green one.

But before I go, a quick cap and polish;
when I smile, wide as a thylacine, I want
to be described as photogenic.

Red Label

In memory of the martyrs of the Athens polytechnic 17/11/73

Johnnie Walker strides out above Piraeus
like the Byron of our days or some
other arrogantly scotched Pom.
The ferry wake churns the port to mist
as we make for Patmos, where St John
(according to the young bloke in the taverna
—a Nick Giannopoulos fan—) had his "Revolution".
It is easy to relax out of history
and into the past instead, aged and amber,
mellow as the tourist and his drink,
comfortable as the patriarch
smoking at Sunday breakfast in jacket and tie,
worry beads at the ready, just in case.
Harder to be the wog boy out of work
in the diaspora or on the broken streets
under Johnnie's well-shod heel.

There's no need for apocalyptic beasts
roaring like minotaurs out of the precious digs,
scaring the suburban charismatics back home.
John's Babylon whore might just as well
be Delta (or any other of Mark Philippoussis' conquests).

And was it Alpha Tau Omega or Sigma Chi,
the frat house that shaped those CIA boys
who made the '67 coup? Richard Welsh,
Bush senior's buddy, came from "Further west
than your sires"Islands of the Blest'."

Now we water our euros till they turn cloudy
and Diogenes flies business class to Brussels,
his lamp a safety hazard, security breach.
So are we all, and worse: unfashionable,
my comrades. Dash down yon glass of scotch and coke.

There are No Kangaroos in Austria

Schloss Hellbrunn, Salzburg

But if there had been in 1615 they would have been here
where all the freaks the Archbishop could gather:
the eight-hoofed horse, the sunflower big as a wheel,
the cleverest dwarf in all Christendom,
danced gawky obeisance to material glory.

Hellbrunn, bright spring, home of weird fish
and pelicans trained not to eat them
by weirder trainers, remains as curiosity,
but in the time of Marcus Sitticus
it was the see to see, the eighth wonder.

Here were the spiritual japes, the sacerdotal
fountains that would squirt holy water
up the bums of guests caught unawares,
baptising them in a fundamental way,
while they got sloshed and schlossed and lost

in mazes, fooled by tricks of the trade, by trade in the tricks
of Church and State, power as means and end.
So the apostolic succession linked
joker to joker, resurrection to rhythm method.
We, deformed, have always been conned or collected.

Elegy for Sandra Dee (1942–2005)

> *"For the first time in my life I don't want to die."*
> — SD 1998

How long a wave could Gidget have ridden
and onto what stretch of grit?
We always expected the prom date promise
to hover like perfume or surf-spray, unfulfilled
but never broken. "Dream Lover"
in the perky bikini that never slipped,
Tammy played opposite the Doctor,
didn't play doctors, but nursed
acned imaginations in every beach cabin
from Malibu to Marrawah.

That exchange when you and Bobby first met:
"I've always enjoyed your pictures, Miss Weld."
"And I always buy your records, Fabian."
You two were our generation's Spencer and Kate.
Now, of course, our generation's
Spencer and Kate are Spencer and Kate,
but when he wrote the songs for you
we sang along; the sand was chaste gold;
the sky was simply blue. Rock 'n' roll
tumbled its innocence into our desire.

The wave eventually breaks.
In the end only purity remains:
an image pure as alcohol, unsullied
as anorexia. The death wish
is wanting never to have turned eight.

Dolphins Off Sikinos

for Matt Simpson

Their leaping surprises but, more,
it's their ease between elements.

On the ferry I'm reading Chomsky on Rice:
"anticipatory self-defense",
how the rule of law's been
"proven inappropriate".
You've got to admire the way her words
slip, cetacean, from liquid lies
to airy nonsense and back.

I have seen her grin. It says,
like the dolphins', "This is fun."

I stumble into grumpy facts,
but on Ios the "Fun Pub" will let me know
that I'm having a good time.
"Have youse finished?" asks
the grim Aussie waitress
and I think, "Not yet. There's still
Straw, Downer and a whole pod
of cavorting diplomats to muse on."

The Death of Reason

When Ratzinger came to Krakow
the city fluttered blue/white,
red/white, yellow/white to greet him;
magic photos taped to windows
blessed every street with the papal gaze.

The Polish Academy of Science
flew a black flag. This city
has mourned before. Three blocks away
oxygen and nitrogen were first
condensed from air. What went wrong?

In the square Mitoraj's *Eros Bendato*,
a hollow human head in bronze,
cast in Lucca (where the inaugural
World Sudoku Championship was held)
has filled with rubbish where the brain would be.

Early Gothic abounds but the miracle
is economic. Early Dylan
plays from the coffee shop. The medieval
market sells tat and T-shirts. I dreamed
I saw St John Paul. I woke up cold.

Roncesvalles: Men at Work

Most on this road are pilgrims,
whether on Ducatis or with staffs,
backpacks and pure expressions.
Pedalling, too, must be hard on the knees.

I don't tote a holy water bottle.
At each shrine I suppress the urge
to give a hoarse rendition
of the Sex Pistols' "I am the Antichrist".

I have climbed, passenger, to this
Pyrenean pass in a hired Astra
(not too arduous) on a pilgrimage
that wears no scallop shell.

The fierce mountain wind
of Puerta de Ibañeta
does not even bring the sound of
Roland's sad horn across the centuries.

It brings cheering in Euskera.
Victory against the invaders,
against the Empire, has the taste
of cherries, of Basque cake, of txakoli.

The familiar silhouette
of the man with the shovel
and that Sisyphean pile of dirt
on the roadside sign makes us slow down.

Unlike that other stick figure
who indicates the Camino
de Santiago de Compostela,
it is a mark of progress.

from *Trainstations from European Poets*

The Bawd, the Lair and Albert Ross

Sue wants to amuse herself with men or their equipment.
She takes Albert Ross, a giant of a man who was overseas
but who's followed the lazy fellow-travellers back home.
He's strong as a navvy, slippery, surly, deep and bitter.

Les is a pain, posing on the boards.
Acts like a king, but he's lazy and malodorous.
It's a shame how Les pits himself against the big whitefellas
as if he's in training for the iron-man contest.

Sue goes for an ale and that's not all she goes for,
lying naked and reading a beaut comic while getting laid,
the one with the big agates at her beck and call.
That's one out of the box if you're weak-willed.

Les assembles a pot and prints out the news.
He's got quick hands and a temper to match.
His ex is sure he's sold millions of them.
Six large ales and he can't even walk.

Do We Know Elly Gee?

Rilke in Australia, early 1970s
for Adi and Irene Wimmer

Hair and "It's Time!": that summer it was so gross
when "Legs" Dynon shat on the sundial.
The winds of change blew through Canberra
a decade late (McMahon, not Macmillan).

You'd feel like listening for a sign;
the Gibbs (Barry and Robin) were in in those days.
We drank while their followers would argue
whether to let Susie swear and whine.

Well, the homeless will always be with us,
and a line (from "Eleanor Rigby"?)
echoes still, among those who stay up late,
lazing and writing letters to the newspapers
which blow back and forth in the alleys and the drives.

An Evening in the Trakl Night Club

Blues or Bach or any fad: Abe and Dan can play it.
You'd fall about; it's a hoot.
They drink like George W. Bush used to, and sometimes
when they're into a kinda meaty blues
they get rotten and balls it up.
Man, they're so professional, but.
You'll see their brows knit in concentration
and their hands pick up the rhythm again
and their fingers are flying like brown leaves in a storm;
they're cooking still!

                      The glance that hurts
the lonely showgirl can, in the dim light,
be taken as flattering; her hair swishes
as she laughs: lucky, tanned and slightly mad.

The shady old crosspatch who runs the joint
flogs the little dolly-bird waitresses
but secretly dreams of being a blues singer.

Andrew, the swankiest patron, an Afro-American banker
with lots of loose gold jewellery
just sighs softly when the stripper comes on.

The lonely girl with chestnut hair understands
that the dark room is symbolic,
that after a night seeking some kind of pleasure
all these strangers—girls, patrons, musos—
have bonded in an ersatz friendship
until they tumble down the stairs to the early sunshine.

Stone No 5: Osip and the Minor Celebrity

Dannii Minogue with a delicate grin
        Taking him down as they're taking him in,

is ready to show you the shadowy sight
        the cops go on hitting till he's got it right.

of the sadness and joy behind her sex appeal.
        Ten minutes they reckon, then he should squeal.

She's a stickler for modesty: keeps her legs low.
        The mongrels have decked him. He goes with the flow.

It's her personality's got her ahead,
        The newsroom will love this; the poor bugger's dead.

pushed her to where she is. (Talent as well!)
        Use your or my logo; the story will sell.

from *A Letter to Egon Kisch* (2007)

from section II

It used to be your mob, of course, dear Egon,
who (or so our leaders would inform us)
threatened a gravity-fed blitzkrieg on
our shores, eager to take our liberty
and our land. Our land! That's an enormous
hole in the collective memory.
Don't let the Mabo case or suchlike fool youse.
There's plenty of mileage yet in *Terra Nullius*.

When I say "your mob", mate, I mean the coms,
the reds, especially the yellow ones,
the ones we had to keep away with bombs.
The bombs weren't really ours; they were the Yanks',
but as they dropped God knows how many tons
our government would offer heartfelt thanks
that they had kept away those fiends from hell,
and offer up young Aussie lives as well.

That was way back in those benighted days
when we would fight in other people's wars.
In this case it was the USA's
(although the tradition goes back to when we helped
our Pommy masters battle with the Boers,
even before Australia was whelped.)
"Benighted," did I say? Those days were dark,
unlike today. Did someone say "Iraq"?

If it's not communists or refugees
it's terrorists with anthrax in their pockets
or evil men with WMDs.
We'll never lack for bogeymen or ogres
to frighten us with guns or bombs or rockets.
One wouldn't need to be as big a rogue as
Saddam or Slobodan to cop the blame,
just have an accent or a funny name.

Our leaders will soon have us cowed and quaking
because it's difference that makes us scared
and fear gives them the go-ahead for making
laws that destroy our freedom. Every time
the TV shows some uniformed, short-haired
efficient thug protecting me from "crime"
I think, Egon, of 1933,
the mantra: "They're not coming after me."

They came all right. They knocked on doors with lists
prepared by snitches, amateur and pro,
of reds and Jews and gays and pacifists
plus a few names that got there by mistake.
(It often happens. No-one's perfect.) So
the *Sturmabteilung*, acting for the sake
of national harmony, dragged off women, men
and children who were never seen again.

We know that it could never happen here.
Australia's a democracy my friend.
Australian citizens don't disappear.
OK, so Immigration gets it wrong
every so often, gets to apprehend,
detain, deport someone who does belong
by right, but is perhaps a trifle "mental".
(It helps a bit if they look oriental.)

We've moved on from the bad old days, of course;
dictation tests in Gaelic are passé.
The largest continent's the largest source
of immigrants these days. We dare no longer
in the words of dear old Arthur Calwell say,
"Two Wongs don't make a white." Your case is stronger
for staying if you've flown in business class.
Jump off a boat and you're out on your arse.

But you, Egon, of all people know that.
A nation of gatekeepers: yeah, that's us.
It's grudgingly we share our habitat.
"We will decide," the little prick once said,
"who comes here and . . ." (beetling his eyebrows thus)
"in what circumstances." If you've fled
from tyranny or torture, jumped a queue
that's non-existent, there's no place for you.

And once you're here you'd better toe the line.
Suppose you've done OK, made a small pile,
while back in Lebanon or Palestine,
wherever it was, there's those left in your wake
who're doin' it hard, and it's just not your style
to say "I'm all right Ahmed" so you make
(to Islamic charities) some small donations.
You'd be advised to check those organisations.

Because the Attorney-General's got a list
(and his list is the only one that matters)
of groups he likes to think are "terrorist".
If you help them, then may Allah help you
'cause no-one here will. You'll be on your pat as
they come to take you for an "interview".
We've thrown habeas corpus out the door ya
know, and you can whistle for a lawyer.

from section VIII

A while back there I wrote about the flag
and how some want to change it: others not.
Of late we've seen how every bronzed ratbag
racist beach bum who's feeling insecure
and thinks that wog-bashing's exactly what
he needs to boost his ego, reassure
himself that he is stronger, whiter, bolder's
not armed until it's draped across his shoulders.

All tried and true flags have a soubriquet:
the "Stars and Stripes", the good old "Union Jack".
Australia's come of age because today
(Forget about that 'roo in boxing gloves.)
no longer does our Aussie banner lack
a nickname, one that everybody loves.
The way our Aussie culture's taking shape,
nothing's more apt than the "Cronulla Cape".

It was that Pommie, Churchill, who once said,
"We'll fight them on the beaches . . ." but the Brits
don't have real beaches. It's our sand runs red
with blood (and, I keep forgetting it, the Turks')
The rallying emblem of all racist shits,
surf club neo-Nazis, loser berks,
One Nation airheads and like-minded dross
is that Blue Ensign with its Southern Cross.

There was a time when public sentiment
was all in favour of a change of flag.
Few tears were shed when our old anthem went,
although a lot would have preferred that song
about jumbucks, a swagman and his swag,
and billies boiling by the billabong,
but it was just too downbeat, I suppose.
"Advance Australia Fair" is what we chose.

But that's about as far as we would go.
Suggest a new flag and the old farts go ape.
"It waved above us when we fought the foe,"
the RSL and hangers-on all thunder.
And so we're stuck with the Cronulla Cape.
It flies to show that we shall never sunder
the ties that bind us to the House of Windsor,
whatever hue our politics or skins are.

Ah, there's the rub: the rub of 15+.
We lie around on beaches to get tanned,
but underneath the skin what makes us us
is our essential whiteness. Dinkum Aussies
get their dark skins from lying on the sand
wearing not much except the briefest cossies.
Bronzed and bonzer? You don't qualify,
if it comes naturally. You have to try.

We've politicians who have made an art
of playing that old game of us and them.
You couldn't call them racist; they're too smart
(except for Danna Vale) to let it show.
They can't afford to have the press condemn
them but they know just how to blow
the dog whistle that, thanks to their cunning,
the racist dogs all hear and so come running.

The white man's burden's what the flag's about.
It stood for "Empire!" everywhere it flew
back when no British colony was without
a Union Jack in its flag's canton. Now
it's us, New Zealand, Fiji, Tuvalu;
the rest have made it clear they won't allow
a foreign flag to dominate. We learn
so slowly, if at all. "Burn, baby, burn!"

Notes

HUSTLER: "Callan Park" was a psychiatric hospital in Sydney, where poet Frank Webb was a patient. Part of it is now the New South Wales Writers' Centre. The "Empress" was the MV *Empress of Australia*, a ferry plying between Balmain and Tasmania.

WHATEVER HAPPENED TO CONWAY TWITTY?: "Stan the Man" was Stan Rofe, one of Australia's first rock 'n' roll radio DJs.

HIGHWAY: DMR = Department of Main Roads

MAN AND LAW: The quotation in stanza 2 is of the opening couplet of Verlaine's "O Triste, Triste Etait Mon Ame" from *Romances Sans Paroles*.

AUTUMN: Valvins was where Mallarmé died.

FIVE TREES: The "Tasman Limited" was a Tasmanian passenger express train.

CLARE: Roger Garaudy (b 1913) was, at the time this poem was written, a French Marxist philosopher. He later converted to Islam and was prosecuted as a Holocaust denier. It is not known whether he still loves the future.

POLHEIM: Wisting smuggled pipe tobacco to the South Pole and offered it to Amundsen as a contribution to the party's celebration of getting there first.

THE WORST JOURNEY IN THE WORLD: See Apsley Cherry-Garrard's book of the same title for a fuller account of this strange expedition.

MAWSON ALONE: Ninnis and Mertz were the other members of this expedition of 1911–12, of which Mawson was the sole survivor. Ninnis fell into a crevasse with six of the dogs. Mawson and Mertz ate the remaining dogs, and for the last hundred miles Mawson pulled the sled with Mertz's corpse back to the base camp.

VANZETTI: It was Judge Thayer who sentenced Sacco and Vanzetti to death for a crime which they patently did not commit.

SONG FOR SEYCHELLES: "The last bearded corsair" was Sir James Mancham, the first President of Seychelles, who spent most of his term of office in luxury in the South of France until deposed by a coup in 1977.

THE ATLAS:

I: "The Battle of Brisbane", November 1942, was between US and Australian servicemen. One Australian was killed and hundreds on both sides injured. It was the Royal Australian Navy that shipped "the bullion to Batavia" in 1946 to fund the attempted restoration of Dutch rule in Indonesia. Colonel Kelly was the officer in charge of the troops who broke the coal miners' strike in Muswellbrook in 1949.

III: "The mountain" is Mt Direction, as viewed from Montrose across the Derwent. Hoess was camp commander at Auschwitz for a time, formerly at Dachau and before that a prisoner himself, having been convicted of murder.

XIV: All the Latin quotations in the first two stanzas are from Cicero's *Pro A. Licinio Archia Poeta Oratio*, delivered in 62 BCE, just a few months after the *In Catilinam* speeches. Lentulus, Cethegus, Gabinius and Statilius were alleged co-conspirators of Catiline who were killed in their cells without trial at the instigation of Cicero. Chick-pea is in Latin *cicero*. "Bradley's" is *Bradley's Arnold*, authoritative Latin grammar textbook. The information on Cowell's biography is from the back-cover blurb of the Pelican edition of his *Cicero and the Roman Republic* (1956). The quotation from the text of the book is from page 234 of that edition. Cowell's conservative bias is patent *passim*.

INTERLUDE: Greystone is the hospital in New York where Woody Guthrie was visited by Bob Dylan in 1961. The second stanza of this interlude is for the voice of Guthrie, the third for that of Dylan.

XVI: The Mannlicher-Carcano 91/38 was the weapon alleged to have been in Lee Harvey Oswald's possession on the day of John Kennedy's assassination.

XIX: The quoted phrases in the fourth stanza are from James McAuley, "For Volunteers Only?", *The Bulletin* 9 April 1966. Bill White was a Victorian teacher who refused to be conscripted and was dragged away from in front of his class and gaoled. For details of the attack on the Man Quang school, see the London *Times*, 18 & 25 March 1965. The phrase, "diggers for dividends" was coined by Clyde Cameron (*Hansard* Vol. 50 p333). "Fairhall's glee" was at the Americans relenting and allowing Australian firms to take part in profiteering from the Vietnam War (see *Hansard* Vol. 50 p21).

ON/AGAINST THE WALL: The "Zanetti Principle" is a method of seeking funding for rural projects by begging enough money from one shire office to buy petrol to drive to the next, and so on. CCDU = Community Cultural Development Unit of the Australia Council for the Arts.

LAUNCHING BY GEORGE: It was suggested at one stage that my book, *Red Dirt*, be launched by George Freeman, a "colourful Sydney identity" and a former acquaintance of the publisher.

SONGS OF THE PROTEST ERA: Song My is the name of the cluster of villages which included My Lai, which was destroyed by American marines in March 1968 when over 300 unarmed civilians, mostly children, were massacred.

ADVICE: Not all Tasmanian police squad cars are white Holden Commodores, but there have been times when it seemed that all white Commodores in the state were police cars.

COMRADE REVENANT: Tommy Jones was an official of the Australian Engineering Union at the Inveresk railway yards in Launceston, which later became the site of the Queen Victoria Museum and Art Gallery. He was also State President of the Communist Party of Australia. The NUR was the National Union of Railwaymen, a phoney organisation set up for the sole purpose of breaking a strike.

THE LAST MUSTER OF THE ABORIGINES AT RISDON: Henry Alken was an English artist of the 18th Century whose works featured aristocrats hunting on horseback. This poem is based on the painting of the same title by John Glover (1836). The following four poems are also based on paintings in the collection of the Queen Victoria Museum and Art Gallery, Launceston: *Low Tide*, William Charles Piguenit (1896); *Fruit and Flowers*, William Buelow Gould (1850), *Sunday in the Gardens*, Ethel Carrick Fox (1907) and *Naming the Sensation* No. 2, Angela Brennan (1995).

NAMING THE SENSATION NO. 2: "JP" is Jackson Pollock.

HUMPTY DUMPTY AND TAXIDERMY: John Wolseley is a visual artist some of whose work is concerned with the botanical and zoological links between Tasmania and Patagonia.

SYDNEY COVE: The *Sydney Cove* was wrecked in Bass Strait in 1797. Campbell and Clark were her shipping agents who, safely on dry land, had remote geographical features named after them in honour of their spirit of enterprise.

LEIPZIG: This poem starts from an incident in 1989 when demonstrators, fleeing from the police who were under orders from the government to shoot to kill (Honecker was the East German President), sought refuge in the Gewandhaus during a concert under the baton of Kurt Masur. As traditionally was supposed to have happened in churches in earlier times, the police declined to pursue them.

TO ADRIAN PAUNESCU: Adrian Paunescu was the official poet of Ceausescu's Romania, which was once the Roman province of Dacia, to which the poet Ovid was exiled. "Tammy" is Tammy Faye Bakker, half of the disgraced American evangelical couple. Alcaeus was a poet of Lesbos in the 6th Century BCE, whose political satires helped depose the tyrant, Melanchros, and bring about a democratic government led by his friend Pittacus. Alcaeus continued to write satires against his (now former) friend and was exiled.

THE LIVING ARE LEFT WITH IMAGINED LIVES: The second stanza contains references to some of Robert Harris's poems. "A million golden birds of future vigor" is a translation of a line by Rimbaud.

ERECHTHEUS 33'S APOLOGIA: This is a response to some of the points made in *Gangland* by Mark Davis (Allen & Unwin 1997).

THE AISLES: The epigraphic line introduces the song, "The Isles of Greece" in *Don Juan*. "Yet in these times he might have done much worse" is part of Byron's appraisal of the song (which, of course, he wrote himself). Hence the reference to irony. "George" is Byron (but it could, at a paronomasial stretch, be Johnston; the cliffs of Hydra are indeed charmin').

BRONTE COUNTRY: Doris Leadbetter, a much underrated performance poet, lived in Haworth before migrating to Australia.

FOR MY FATHER: "Seeking heroics, we become absurd" is from "Home Movies", published in my first book, *Tense Mood and Voice*, (Lyre-Bird Writers 1969).

OOSUTORARIA: ". . . sang like kangaroos" refers to the poem by Henry Newbolt on the WWI battle between the *Sydney* and the *Emden* which contains the lines (referring to the Australian sailors): "Their hearts were hot / and as they shot / they sang like kangaroos." It was the Cascade brewery that "got its tail wrong on the labels" of their Premium Lager, but they can hardly be blamed, as they use a copy of the famous Gould painting which wrongly gives the thylacines striped tails. Fairlie Arrow was a minor pop singer of the 1980s who faked her own kidnapping as a publicity stunt. The Last Resort was a bar in Katoomba.

VINEGAR HILL: There is no actual Vinegar Hill in NSW. The 1804 uprising (the subject of this poem) took its name from the uprising in Wexford, Ireland, in 1798. "General" Joseph Holt, one of the leaders of the Wexford rebellion, had a change of heart during his transportation, but was locked up anyway, then exiled to Norfolk Island. He was later pardoned and returned to Ireland. Phillip Cunningham, the Irish leader, was bludgeoned by the Quartermaster, Thomas

Laycock, left for dead, then picked up and hanged without a trial. James Ruse was transported for burglary, and became the first successful farmer in the colony. "Natef of Cornwell" is part of his tombstone inscription. As is common among natives of Cornwall, he was of short stature.

SPIDER DANCE AND HORSE WHIP: Lola Montez won a horse whip in a raffle in Ballarat and joked that she would use it on the newspaper editor in response to his moralistic fulminations against her.

MANDARIN OF THE CRYSTAL BUTTON: The incident described in the first stanza took place in 1888. Ninny Melville was a NSW politician and Ezra Norton a newspaper editor. Henry Parkes, Premier of NSW, defied British law and the wishes of other colonial leaders to bring in the first regulations restricting Chinese immigration. Quong Tart was killed in 1903.

CONINGHAM V CONINGHAM: "Moran missed out on precedence" to which, by virtue of his seniority, he would have been entitled, given that the Church of England could expect no privileged treatment in the new nation.

LOCKOUT: John Brown was the manager of the Rothbury mine at the time of the lockout. "Our Norm" was Norm Brown (needless to say, no relation), the only direct fatality.

THE MAYOR: The character Ron Lassiter in Hardy's *Power Without Glory* was allegedly based on a real Mayor of Richmond, Victoria, Con Loughnan. Loughnan was, however, Mayor in 1932 and the visit of the Gloucesters was in 1934. The three main factions in the Victorian ALP at the time were those controlled by John Wren, the Left and the Catholic Right (led by Stanley Keon and later to break away and become the DLP). "Squizzy" Taylor was a notorious Melbourne gangster and associate of Loughnan's.

TANAH MERAH: Tanah Merah was an internment camp established by the Dutch for political prisoners on the Digul River in what is now West Papua. Fred Paterson, State MP for Bowen, was the only Communist ever to be elected to any Australian parliament. Mynheer Dr Charles Van Der Plas was the last representative in Australia of the Netherlands East Indies Commission.

ADVENT: 21 DEC. 1967: St Paul's Cathedral, Melbourne, was the site of the memorial service for Harold Holt, the Australian Prime Minister who had been missing, presumed drowned in the surf of Cheviot Beach, Portsea, since 17 December. Tet is the Vietnamese New Year (in February by our calendar).

SIGHT SCREEN: Kim Hughes had wept on losing the captaincy of the Australian cricket team. He went to play in South Africa despite the boycott which many sporting bodies and individuals observed during the later years of Apartheid.

ET IN ACADIA EGO?: Acadia was the name for the French settled parts of the Canadian Maritime Provinces, an area which, despite the title's play on words, only partly resembles the classical Arcadia of the original Latin tag. Bill Guthro, we can safely assume, survived the incident, which occurred in July 2000. Andrew Hardy, a poet of great promise who died at the age of 23, was allegedly responsible for a series of stencilled graffiti in the streets of Launceston, including a picture of a man with a rifle and the slogan "I protect family values", and another which read, "Think long and connected".

MESOPOTAMIAN SUITE: The statue of Scheherazade in Baghdad, unlike that of Saddam Hussein, survived the US led invasion of 2003. "The voting bit has been taken out": this was before the occupying forces relented under Shiite pressure and agreed to elections. The Baghdad Poetry Festival had been one of the world's biggest.

SOUTH-WESTERN BAPTIST: Paige Patterson was the head of South-Western Baptist University, and, during his vacations, a big-game hunter in Africa.

MEDITATIONS ON MS WESTBURY'S PRECEPTS: The italicised lines are from "Metaphor in Poetry", Deborah Westbury, in *The Writer's Reader* (Halstead Press, 2002) pp. 148, 149.

DENTIST'S WAITING ROOM: Terri Schiavo was the woman in a coma who became a cause célèbre for the extreme christian right in 2006. *Ten Days on the Island* is a biennial arts festival held in Tasmania, where the use of the poison 1080 against native fauna is common.

RED LABEL: There is a 20 storey high billboard advertising Johnnie Walker whisky on the waterfront of Piraeus. Nick Giannopoulos is an Australian actor of Greek background who starred in *Wogs Out of Work*. "Delta" is Delta Goodrem, singer, actor and minor celebrity. Richard Welsh, CIA station chief in Greece, was executed (or assassinated, depending on your point of view) in December 1975. "Further west / than your sires' 'Islands of the Blest'" is a quote from Byron's "Isles of Greece" song in Canto III of *Don Juan*, to the last line of which this poem's last line also refers.

ELEGY FOR SANDRA DEE: Two of Sandra Dee's movies were *Gidget* and *Tammy and the Doctor*. Her husband, singer Bobby Darin, wrote and recorded "Dream Lover". "Spencer and Kate" are Tracy and Hepburn; I once had to explain this to a successful movie director. Sandra Dee was sexually assaulted at the age of eight.

THE DEATH OF REASON: "When Ratzinger came to Krakow" was May 2006. The colours in the first stanza refer to the flags of the city of Krakow, of Poland and of the Vatican, in that order.

RONCESVALLES: MEN AT WORK: It was the Basques (not, as in the *Chanson de Roland*, the Moors) who attacked Charlemagne's army during its retreat from Spain in 778. Euskera is the native language of the Basques. Txakoli is a sharpish white wine from the region. Part of the highway across the Pyrenees near Roncesvalles runs parallel to the famous pilgrims' walking track, the Camino de Santiago de Compostela.

TRAINSTATIONS FROM EUROPEAN POETS: Train stations are places from which you are taken elsewhere. The poems originated from the following stations (in order): "L'Albatros" by Charles Baudelaire; "Herbsttag" by Rainer Maria Rilke; "Am Abend" by Georg Trakl; "Stone" Part 5, by Osip Mandelstam.

A LETTER TO EGON KISCH: Egon Kisch, a Czech national and a Jew, had been deported from Nazi Germany in 1933. He travelled the world, speaking and writing on important political issues, coming to Australia in 1934 at the invitation of the Movement Against War and Fascism. The Australian Government, through Attorney-General Robert Menzies and Immigration Minister Eric Harrison, refused him entry. Kisch jumped off his ship to the Port Melbourne wharf, breaking his leg in the process, and challenged the ban in the courts. He won and spent four months here. His book, *Australian Landfall*, published in 1937, remains one of the most perceptive and entertaining accounts of this country. After living in Mexico for several years, Egon Kisch died in Czechoslovakia in 1948.

The "little prick" is otherwise known as "the lying little rodent". Danna Vale was a minister in his government who, in February 2005, said that Australians were "aborting themselves almost out of existence" and that Australia would be a Muslim nation in 50 years.